everyday psalms

May the Blessings of Easter
be with you every day of
the year.
We love you —
Kevin + Theresa
4-19-14

everyday psalms

MEDITATIONS FOR LIVING THE LORD'S SONGS

ALAN J. HOMMERDING

EVERYDAY PSALMS
150 Meditations for Living the Lord's Songs

Author: Alan J. Hommerding
Editor: Michael E. Novak
Production Editor: Mary Brewick
Copy Editor: Marcia T. Lucey
Cover and Book Design: Chris Broquet
Director of Publications: Mary Beth Kunde-Anderson
Production Manager: Deb Johnston

WLP 001759
ISBN 978-1-58459-433-8

World Library Publications
3708 River Road, Suite 400
Franklin Park, IL 60131-2158

introduction

I thought I knew the psalms, until one hot mid-July day when I was sitting with my mother in the kitchen of her house. We had just returned from a difficult visit to see my father at the nursing home. He hadn't known us at all that day, and when we three had sat out in the garden he had shown no interest in anything, not even the flowers and birds that usually fascinated him. We didn't speak it out loud, but that was the day we knew the next life awaited him, and soon. Looking out the kitchen window, tears in her eyes, my mother sang, with a catch in her throat, "This is the day the Lord has made. Let us rejoice and be glad." I knew the psalm refrain from Easter Sunday, and had even written a musical setting of it; but how much more I came to know it in that quietly remarkable moment, a moment very much in need of Easter. My father passed away within the month. Having come to know the psalms a bit better, I was able to pray through my own tears, "This is the day the Lord has made. Let us rejoice and be glad."

I thought I knew the psalms, until one day I happened across a reference to the snake charmer and deaf cobra of Psalm 58. Even though I had read the Bible through a number of times, and by that particular point in time I had been through the Sunday psalter of the three years of the Roman Catholic Lectionary more than ten times, I did not remember this colorful reference! I knew that the Lectionary omitted certain verses of psalms, so I went to check it out, and discovered that Psalm 58 wasn't in the Sunday Lectionary psalter at all. Neither were Psalms 11, 14, 20, 35, 38, 39, 53, 64, 70, 73, 75, 76, 83, 108, 120, 125, 129, 133, 134, 140, or 142. This doesn't mean, of course, that the theology or themes of these psalms weren't in the Lectionary. There is a substantial amount of repetition in the psalter; Israel's singers and the Holy Spirit drew on their common heritage as they responded to the changing circumstances of their communities' lives. This is characteristic of our own spiritual formation as well. (If we could learn it and live it after one encounter, we wouldn't need an entire psalter!) Lectionaries, however, are meant to be invitations into the fullness of God's word, and so I wondered what else I might have missed by thinking that this invitation was the whole celebration.

I decided I would take my own deeper look into the psalter. As a spiritual exercise, I chose one verse from each psalm every day, meditated on it a bit, wrote a brief reflection and a prayer, and gave myself one activity to do that day that would help me embody the psalm verse. The fruits of that exercise were the starting point of this collection of one-minute meditations. Later on, I decided that I would search for all the ways that Israel's psalmists continued to sing in the Christian scriptures. More often than not, the psalm verse I had worked with would take me somewhere that the Lectionary didn't go with the same psalm. Other times, it did. But it was another way for the changing face of daily life to be enriched by the persistent, grace-filled themes of the psalms.

These meditations are meant to be an invitation, an example of one way to delve further into the treasures of God's word. The individual verses are not meant to be a "theme" or a one-line reduction of an entire psalm, but merely one more way in. I hope you will come to know, live, and sing the gifts of the psalter a bit better, and also come to know how inexhaustible its riches are.

Take time with these meditations, allowing the wisdom of the psalms to seep into your life slowly. This is more important than getting through the entire book within a given time frame. One per day, at most!

As you enter into these reflections, prayers, and actions, may you know that this day, each day, is made by the Lord. Rejoice and be glad!

Alan J. Hommerding

PSALM 1:6

The Lord watches over the way of the righteous,
but the way of the wicked will perish.

We might think that the opposite of "wicked" is "good."
But the scriptures offer us a different option: righteousness.
Acting righteously, in right relationship with the will of God
and rightly toward others, is an active way of living, not merely
a passive state of goodness. How often is our passivity really
the wickedness of inaction? The scriptures have no time for
those who are self-righteous, because the reign of God calls
us to be God-righteous.

PRAYER

Your will be done on earth as in heaven,
O God our Father.
Keep me steadfast and faithful in your way,
turning away from wickedness,
living righteously.

LIVING THE PRAYER

Today I will act to bring God's righteousness into the world.
Most days offer some opportunity, a fork in the road,
to choose between acting righteously or staying inactive.
When has such an opportunity recently presented itself?
Did I choose the righteous way?

THE NEW TESTAMENT SINGS

Jesus said . . . "I am the way, and the truth, and the life.
No one comes to the Father except through me."
(John 14:6)

PSALM 2:10

Now therefore, O kings, be wise;
be warned, O rulers of the earth.

It is easy to think that this psalm isn't speaking to us. "I'm not a king. I'm not a ruler." Perhaps we need to think of ourselves in this instance as the psalmist, the one offering the cautionary note to kings and rulers, speaking with the voice of God who scorns the folly of nations that turn away from God's reign for the sake of their own. The psalmist acts as a prophet "speaking up" in public for the voiceless, the poor, and the outcast. Not caving in to despair or cynicism, the psalmist/prophet speaks out in prayer and action.

PRAYER

Help me listen, O Lord, for your wisdom.
May I speak out boldly
in whatever ways I can,
and use the life you have given
to speak your truth.

LIVING THE PRAYER

Today I will truly hear God's wisdom and speak in a way that allows others to hear it.
How can I speak out in my life to awaken leadership to following the ways of God? What can I work for, so that those named "blessed" in the Beatitudes will know God's love for them?

THE NEW TESTAMENT SINGS

I urge that supplications, prayers, intercessions, and thanksgivings be made for everyone, for kings and all who are in high positions, so that we may lead a quiet and peaceable life in all godliness and dignity.
(1 Timothy 2:1–2)

10

PSALM 3:5

I lie down and sleep;
I wake again, for the LORD sustains me.

Scriptural tradition holds that David wrote this psalm while he was fleeing from his son Absalom and other enemies. Even in this time of trial ("stress," we'd call it today) David doesn't lose any sleep. His trust in the Lord's sustaining power is such that it allows him to sleep while enemies are in pursuit, and he also realizes that divine power is what allows him to wake each day. Does our faith allow us to slumber peacefully? Or are we kept awake wondering how we (not God) will handle the trials of our life?

PRAYER

Keep me confident
in your sustaining power, Lord.
Refresh and strengthen me
so I may face each day renewed by your love,
and act according to your will.

LIVING THE PRAYER

Today I will resolve a troublesome spot in my life by turning it over to God.
What stressful situation am I facing today? Without caving in to irresponsibility, how can I find ways to combine faith in God with responsible and effective means of dealing with life's circumstances?

THE NEW TESTAMENT SINGS

The Son is the radiance of God's glory and true image of God, sustaining all things by his powerful word.
(Hebrews 1:3)

PSALM 4:6

There are many who say,
"O that we might see some good!
Let the light of your face shine on us, O LORD!"

Ancient Israel had a deep and potent personal relationship with God, and the language of personal encounter imbues their writings. Yet for the Israelites, seeing the face of God was a frightening proposition: nobody could look upon God's face and live. But the countenance of God was life-giving; it was considered a source of blessing, light, and (in this passage) goodness itself. Only in one context could one look upon the face of God and live: when called to life eternal.

PRAYER

God of life eternal,
let your face shine upon me.
Watch over me, guide me;
with your tender gaze bless me
all the days of my life.

LIVING THE PRAYER

Today I will be a source of the light of God's face for someone by doing good.
Can I see the irony in saying that I would like to see some good happen in the world, but doing nothing to help it happen? Who has seen God's face in my face or deeds?

THE NEW TESTAMENT SINGS

Blessed are the pure in heart, for they will see God.
(Matthew 5:8)

PSALM 5:11

Let all who find refuge in you be glad;
  let them always sing with joy.
Shelter them;
  may all those who love your name rejoice in you.

The people of ancient Israel were a people who wandered, who lived as nomadic tribes or in exile, even a people who— when settled—spent much time outdoors in the fields, with herds, on the way to market, or to fetch water. For them shelter was a big deal, whether it was refuge from the elements or enemies. People who are victims of natural disasters understand this, but many of us don't live this way. Nevertheless, there are many things in life from which all of us need "shelter" from time to time. God, for us, is still that shelter.

PRAYER

Shelter me, O Lord,
keep me safe, protect me.
Let me always rejoice in you,
my refuge.

LIVING THE PRAYER

Today I will allow the Lord to be my refuge.
Can I spare a few moments to think about what I may need to be sheltered from? Is one of them the busy-ness that doesn't allow "a few moments"? How can God be my shelter? How will I rejoice?

THE NEW TESTAMENT SINGS

The Lord is faithful; the Lord will strengthen and protect you from the evil one.
(2 Thessalonians 3:3)

PSALM 6:6

I am worn out from moaning;
>I flood my pillow with weeping all night,
>I soak my bed with tears.

This is an example of the psalms' "don't hold back" approach to prayer. The psalmist finds it nearly impossible to overstate how miserable life is ("I make my bed swim in tears," one translation has it). Technically, this way of speaking or writing is called hyperbole, but in the psalms it's used as a means to express utmost trust, confidence, and intimacy, all in an honest, loving relationship with God. With whom do we share our most extreme moments of any emotion? With those we love the most, with whom we are most at ease, and whom we rely on above all others.

PRAYER

I place all my trust in you,
loving and faithful God.
I place before you all that lies deep in my heart.
Hear and answer this and every prayer.

LIVING THE PRAYER

Today I will express a joy or sorrow to God "one step further" than I normally would.
Do I follow in the way of Israel and Jesus, who pray confidently, intimately to a loving "Abba" and show us to do the same?
Do I pray as one assured of the close, loving relationship I have with God?

THE NEW TESTAMENT SINGS

Father, if you are willing, take this cup away from me; but let not my will, but yours be done.
(Luke 22:42)

PSALM 7:14

Sinners conceive trouble,
  they are pregnant with wickedness,
  they give birth to lies.

There is no greater physical connection between two human
beings than that of a pregnant mother and her child.
The psalmist uses this very potent metaphor to describe how
what we bear in our spiritual "wombs" is what we will,
ultimately, give birth to. It is a consistent theme of the
scriptures: what is in our hearts is known only to God while
it is there, but it will, eventually, be "born" in our actions.
Today we might think of this image this way: if we were to get
a spiritual sonogram, would it show a healthy child?

PRAYER

You see into my depths, O Lord.
Help me to search my life
so that it will be truly pleasing to you.

LIVING THE PRAYER

Today I will ask God to cleanse me, so my deeds will be filled with
life and goodness.
Do I use the spiritual discipline "examination of conscience"
or some other to scrutinize those parts of my life that need to
be healthier? When is the last time I did some sort of spiritual
examination?

THE NEW TESTAMENT SINGS

Likewise, your good deeds will be quite evident, while those that
are not cannot be concealed.
(1 Timothy 5:25)

PSALM 8:2

From the mouths of babes and infants
      you have raised a fortress,
      a defense to silence your enemies and avengers.

*It is easy to read this verse as a mere sentimental statement
about how much God loves children. But here the psalmist is
using an extreme paradox to illustrate God's power and God's
ability to wield power everywhere. In Israel's society, babes and
infants were not only physically weak and helpless, their social
standing was zero, since their future was not assured, given the
high mortality rate. Yet God can use even them to build up a
defense, and can vanquish enemies through them. How often do
we think we are too insignificant or helpless to be a source for
God's power in the world? Not so!*

PRAYER

> Mighty God,
> we all are weak and lowly before you.
> Let me, your child,
> show forth your reign in the world.

LIVING THE PRAYER

*Today I will be confident that God has chosen me to conquer
whatever works against the divine will.*
Who are the "zero status" people in our world? The world
at large? How is God's power being displayed through them?
Through me?

THE NEW TESTAMENT SINGS

"If you humble yourself, as this child, then you shall be
greatest in the kingdom of heaven."
(Matthew 18:4)

PSALM 9:3

When my enemies retreat,
     they stumble and perish before you, LORD God.

This is another one of David's war songs. Ancient Israel, like its neighbors, placed its God in the midst of its military dealings. What remains at the forefront of Israel's prayer is that victory is sought only so that the justice and righteousness of Israel's God can be fulfilled. And it was always clear that, when there is victory, it is God's. This verse states it succinctly: when my enemies retreat, they retreat before you, God. It's more practical for us to think of the smaller battles we wage in daily life, but to remember always that our strength to do so comes from God, and God is always the victor.

PRAYER

I will turn to you, Lord my strength,
in all that I may confront today.
Let me seek your justice
and do your will.

LIVING THE PRAYER

Today I will give credit for a life "victory" to God and not to myself.
What will I encounter today that seems like a battle? Does it truly need to be one? Is it more important that I win or that God's justice and loving-kindness are known?

THE NEW TESTAMENT SINGS

Whoever is truly born of God conquers the world. This is the victory that has conquered the world: our faith.
(1 John 5:4)

PSALM 10:12

Arise, O Lord! Lift up your hand, O God.
Do not forget the powerless.

Don't make promises you can't keep. Keep your promises. From time to time, Israel felt a need to remind God of the promises that had been made with them in the covenant, to prod God out of inactivity, perhaps to wake God from a slumber. But to wake a God who seems to be asleep can be a dangerous thing. The God of the covenant, who is perfect faithfulness and love, does keep promises. But a covenant was—and is—a two-way contract. The God who arises to lift a mighty hand on behalf of the powerless can, likewise, turn to us and say, "Now you arise, now you lift a hand to help the powerless."

PRAYER

Let me arise with you,
loving and faithful God,
to lift my hand for those
who are poor and weak.

LIVING THE PRAYER

Today as I lift up my hands in prayer, I will also help— instead of hurt—others.
We are inundated with news stories of the plight of the helpless in our society and around the world. Does this make me feel helpless? Or am I lifted up by God's power to try and make a difference?

THE NEW TESTAMENT SINGS

When Jesus saw the crowds, he was moved with pity. They were troubled and helpless, like sheep without a shepherd. (Matthew 9:36)

PSALM 11:3
If the foundations are in ruins,
what can the upright do?

Anyone who's ever experienced an earthquake, even a minor one, knows how helpless one feels while it is going on. It comes up quite quickly, and there is no way or nowhere to get away from it. As our knowledge of the earth increases, we have come to learn that things we perceive as stable are actually quite unstable. This certainly happens in life, when those things or people we have counted on will unexpectedly shake us up. Sometimes that part of our life ends up in ruins. The psalmist, in a curious turn of phrase, will remind us that our true foundation is God's throne set in heaven.

PRAYER

I lift my hands
to your throne of grace, O Lord.
Help me find my strength
and security only there.

LIVING THE PRAYER

Today I will be a source of God's strength for someone whose life has been shaken up.
Would I stand on a chair with casters to reach something fragile on a high shelf? What "stable" things in my life would leave me feeling helpless if they were ruined? How would I turn to God?

THE NEW TESTAMENT SINGS

Jesus said to them, "Destroy this temple, and I will raise it up in three days."
(John 2:19)

PSALM 12:8

The wicked freely strut about
when people honor what is vile.

We can only "strut our stuff" when the context of life allows us to, or when we have an audience. To get dressed up in elegant formal wear, jewels, and so on, to go "strut your stuff" in the grocery store would be silly. It's the wrong context. So when we see the wicked (or the vain, or the prideful, or the thoughtless) able to strut about freely and successfully, perhaps we need not criticize them, but critique ourselves and our communities for providing or allowing the circumstances in which their activites are promoted or admired.

PRAYER
....
Lord, help me honor and treasure
what is good and right,
so that I may humbly walk with you.

LIVING THE PRAYER

Today I will turn away from or "turn off" those who abuse their status, wealth, popularity, or power.
What do I honor that is vile? If not vile, what do I honor that is not healthy for my spiritual life? What do I value that is contrary to the gospel?

THE NEW TESTAMENT SINGS

God has scattered the proud in the imagination of their hearts. (Luke 1:51)

PSALM 13:1

How long, O LORD? Will you forget me forever?
How long will you hide your face from me?

*When the psalmists began with a question, it was often a cue
to God that a complaint was coming up. A psalm that opens
this way is usually categorized as a "lament" but that word
does a disservice, especially if we think that it just means
"sad" or implies passivity. The laments are by turns questioning,
challenging, angry; the psalmists can get a bit smart-alecky
with God, this one even accusing God of hiding, not having
the courage to look the psalmist "in the face." But we must
recall that expressing these feelings is one more way to show
trust in God.*

PRAYER

Show me your face, O Lord;
do not hide, but show me your will,
so that I may come to know it
and live it better.

LIVING THE PRAYER

*Today I will love and trust God enough to ask a deeply honest
or challenging question.*
We often ask "How can a loving God allow . . . ?"
Do I ask this only of others, or do I dare ask it of God?

THE NEW TESTAMENT SINGS

God, who said, "Let there be light!" made light to shine in our
hearts, giving us the light of knowledge of God's glory in the face
of Christ.
(2 Corinthians 4:6)

PSALM 14:3

All have turned aside from the LORD,
together they become corrupt;
there is no one who does what is good,
not even one.

There is a story about a proud parent who, as the marching band passes by, exclaims, "Look! Everyone is out of step except my kid!" When our prayer takes on an accusatory tone about the waywardness of others, it is probably a good time to ask if we, too, have gone astray. Corruption, like misery or any number of other human activities, loves company. When we say "there is no one who does what is good" we ought not be thinking "there is no one—except me—who does what is good." The good news is that honesty and integrity can also begin with one person: me.

PRAYER

When I stray,
help me find my way back to you,
faithful God.
Let me live as a sign of your goodness.

LIVING THE PRAYER

Today I will examine my own actions before I criticize others.
Whom do I criticize most often out of pride or jealousy or insecurity? Is that person truly bad, or am I critical so I can make myself feel better?

THE NEW TESTAMENT SINGS

"How can you see the speck in someone else's eye, but fail to notice the plank that is in yours?"
(Matthew 7:3)

PSALM 15:1

Lord, who may abide in your tent?
Who may dwell on your holy mountain?

One of the other uses of initial questions in the psalms,
in addition to inaugurating a lament ("How long, O Lord?"),
is to set up a teaching moment, like in a catechism. Psalm 15
starts by asking who may attain the greatest prize of all:
to live as one with God, as in the tent of the Ark of the Covenant
or on Sinai, both crucial places for covenant faith. Since the
prize is so great, it is no wonder that the answer is so rigorous.
The one who lives a deeply honest, upright life can attain this prize.

PRAYER

Keep me true to you
and righteous in my deeds, Lord.
Bring me to live with you forever.

LIVING THE PRAYER

Today I will keep my "eyes on the prize" by acting rightly and
justly toward all others.
Can I, even for one day, do what is righteous? Always speak
the heartfelt truth? Not slander or lie about others? Keep my
promises? Give without expecting a little extra in return?

THE NEW TESTAMENT SINGS

" 'I tell you truly, whatever you did not do for one of the least of
these, you did not do it for me.' Then they will go away to eternal
punishment, but the righteous to eternal life."
(Matthew 25:45–46)

23

PSALM 16:3

As for the saints in the land, they are noble;
in them is all my delight.

*If a passerby asked you "What is a saint?" what would your
answer be? For Israel, the saints (or the holy ones, or the godly)
weren't only good people, or holy people, or people whom God
loved—though they were all those things—they were living and
tangible manifestations of the very presence of God, like the
Torah or the temple. Paul and the early church called all the
baptized "saints." Who is a saint in your life, that godly person
who reminds you of God's eternal, faithful love, challenging you
to live in a godly manner? Who delights in you as a saint?*

PRAYER

Source of all holiness,
let me see your presence
in all those around me,
and help me live a saintly life.

LIVING THE PRAYER

Today I will be more aware of God's presence in others.
Who has shown me God's unfailing love in a holy way?
To whom have I been a sign of that same kind of divine love?
Can I also find God's holy presence in unexpected people
and places?

THE NEW TESTAMENT SINGS

Here, then, is the steadfastness of the saints who keep God's
commands and faith in Jesus.
(Revelation 14:12)

PSALM 17:8

Keep me as the apple of your eye;
hide me in the shadow of your wings.

The "apple" of God's eye in this verse is the pupil: the eye's center, its heart. When we ask this of God, we are not merely asking to be seen as the good boy or good girl whom God loves; we are expressing belief that God's love is so great that we are always kept there. The psalm also uses the image of the mother bird that, on a nest or on the ground, is sheltering her fragile, helpless chicks with her wings. How great yet gentle is God's love for us!

PRAYER

Keep me, hide me,
shelter me, hold me,
God of tender, eternal love.

LIVING THE PRAYER

Today I will realize how fragile I am, how much I need God's love for me.
If I truly am at the center of God's eye, what does God see in my daily living? If, like the mother bird, God shelters me, do I accept that or try to go off on my own?

THE NEW TESTAMENT SINGS

I am convinced that neither death, nor life, nor angels, nor principalities, nor things here present or things to come, nor powers, nor the heights or depths, nor any created thing, will separate us from the love of God, which is in Christ Jesus our Lord. (Romans 8:38–39)

PSALM 18:27

You save the humble,
> and you bring low those whose eyes are proud.

*According to tradition and manuscript inscriptions, David
sang this psalm when God delivered him from his enemies,
from the hand of his main enemy, King Saul. David, then, is
singing of himself as the humble one, and of Saul as being proud.
Since Saul was king of Israel and messiah—the anointed one of
God—David is saying something quite radical: even those who
have been anointed for positions of authority by God can become
sinful and proud, and ultimately be brought low again by God.
This was a lesson David would have done well to remember later
on in his life.*

PRAYER

God of all power,
keep me honest and humble.
May I never act proudly,
but live always as a servant.

LIVING THE PRAYER

*Today I will do something for others that might be considered
"beneath" me.*
What kind of power or authority do I have in my life,
even of the simplest sort? Do I use it humbly, as a servant of God
and others, or am I proud when I can exercise my status?

THE NEW TESTAMENT SINGS

God has brought down the rulers from their thrones, and has
exalted those who are humble.
(Luke 1:52)

PSALM 19:14

May the words of my mouth, and the meditations of my heart
    be acceptable to you,
    O Lord, my Rock and my Redeemer.

*It might seem more logical for this, the final verse of the psalm,
to come at the beginning, before the psalmist is going to speak
or meditate. Even today, many Jewish rites put these words at
the end of a prayer or time of meditation, as a summary or
consecration. These words, and their place in this psalm, can be
a helpful reminder that—though we prepare ourselves with the
best intentions—it is possible for us to wander away from God's
path, even in prayer.*

PRAYER

I lift my prayers to you,
Lord my God.
Guide my every word,
thought, and deed.

LIVING THE PRAYER

*Today I will begin and conclude at least one moment of prayer
with dedication of myself to God.*
How do I pray? Do I only use memorized prayers? Do I always
try to be spontaneous? Is my praying only a relentless list of
my personal needs? Can I also selflessly embrace the joys and
desires of the world around me?

THE NEW TESTAMENT SINGS

During his earthly life, Jesus offered up prayers and petitions with
loud cries and tears to the one who could save him from death,
and he was heard because of his reverence.
(Hebrews 5:7)

PSALM 20:4

May God grant you your heart's desire,
and make all of your plans succeed.

What a beautiful and simple wish this psalm verse contains!
Its simplicity might fool us into believing that God grants our
heart's desire to win the lottery or makes our plan to be voted
"most popular" a success. Before God grants us anything, or
makes any part of our life successful, it has to be in union with
the will of God. This happens more often when we have also
granted the desires of God's heart, and when we strive to make
God's plan for the world succeed. This keeps us from thinking
wrongly that prayer gives us some sort of remote control of God.

PRAYER

You know my every desire,
you see my every plan, O Lord.
Help me to walk in your ways,
for you alone bring joy to my life.

LIVING THE PRAYER

Today I will evaluate my desires and my plans for life.
Are the things that I desire or the goals that I strive to attain
truly of God? What might be God's other desires and plans
for me?

THE NEW TESTAMENT SINGS

For human anger does not bring about the righteous life,
the life that God desires.
(James 1:20)

PSALM 21:1

O Lord, the king rejoices in your strength.
How great is his joy in the victories you give!

*Though this psalm is royal in its exaltation of the king
(David), it begins with—and retains—a prophetic focus:
we are not strong, God is; we are not victorious, God is. This
hearkens back to Moses keeping the staff of God raised so that
Israel might be victorious (Exodus 17:8). This kind of humble
acknowledgment of God's power is an observance of the first
commandment. We cannot give God's place in our lives to
anything or anybody, even ourselves. As we turn to God in times
of trouble or disappointment, we also turn to God in times of
personal triumph or happiness.*

PRAYER

God of power and might,
all that I count as success
is graciously granted by you;
I will glorify you alone.

LIVING THE PRAYER

Today I will name and credit God for a success or blessing in my life.
Do I fall into the pattern of only turning to God in times
of need or sorrow? What thing that I count as a personal
achievement actually occurred because I discerned and
obeyed God's will?

THE NEW TESTAMENT SINGS

Thanks be to God, who gives us the victory through Jesus Christ
our Lord.
(1 Corinthians 15:57)

PSALM 22:9

You brought me safely from my mother's womb;
you led me to trust you while at her breast.

*The opening line of this psalm is one of the most famous psalm
quotes in the Gospels. Matthew and Mark place it on Jesus' lips
as he dies on the cross. It is generally accepted that, in doing so,
they were depicting Christ praying the entire psalm, not just
the opening line (the same as using "Our Father" to indicate
the whole Lord's Prayer). Jesus, in the ultimate moment of
abandonment, was also praying and keeping his faith focused
on the total love and faithfulness of God, in which he trusted
from the moment he came from Mary's womb and nursed at
her breast.*

PRAYER

I trust in you, my God;
you have been with me
and known me every moment,
every day of my life.
Keep me faithful to you always.

LIVING THE PRAYER

*Today I will recall a moment that God was with me, even when
I felt alone.*
How have God's love and faithfulness been present in my life
from the very beginning? Have I returned the favor? In what
ways can God trust in me?

THE NEW TESTAMENT SINGS

Do not let your hearts be troubled. Have trust in God, trust also
in me.
(John 14:1)

PSALM 23:2

The LORD makes me lie down in green pastures;
he leads me beside peaceful waters.

*The core image of this psalm—God as shepherd, us as sheep—
is not terribly flattering to us. Sheep are not very bright, are
largely defenseless, and left to their own devices, would likely
perish or be devoured. They sometimes need to be forced to green
pastures because they prefer the over-grazed, barren land with
which they are familiar. An unflattering image, perhaps,
but not completely inaccurate. We, too, sometimes prefer the
malnutrition of familiarity or the turbulent waters that seem
to give life some sort of movement. Fortunately, if we heed the
voice of the shepherd, we are led to a better place.*

PRAYER
Shepherd me in your love, my Lord.
Lead me to places
refreshing and restoring,
so that I may follow you all my days.

LIVING THE PRAYER
*Today, in humility, I will ask God to lead me from a place where I
should not be.*
How convinced am I that I always know what's best? Do I
truly listen for the Shepherd's voice? When I hear it, do I
humbly follow, or stubbornly stay where I am?

THE NEW TESTAMENT SINGS
I am the good shepherd; I know my sheep and they know me.
(John 10:14)

PSALM 24:7

Lift up your heads, O gates;
be lifted up, O ancient doors;
let the King of glory enter in.

Whether we think of the gates and doors in this psalm as representing those of a temple sanctuary or those of our own hearts, we might want to be a little careful about opening up for the King of glory to enter. What will the King find inside? The gates and doors are also emblems of the entry to God's eternal reign, that place for those of clean hands and pure hearts who have lived on behalf of the least and lowly. Is that what the King of glory will find? Or will some housecleaning have to be done?

PRAYER

I open the gates of my heart
and the doorway to my life
to you, my loving God.
May you find your reign
of peace and justice therein.

LIVING THE PRAYER

Today I will make my life a true dwelling place for the King of glory.
What sort of clutter or outright dirt is in my spiritual house? In the house of prayer where I worship? How can I clean up my own life and help others do so as well?

THE NEW TESTAMENT SINGS

Jesus said: "It is written 'My house will be a house of prayer' but you have turned it into a den for thieves."
(Luke 19:46)

PSALM 25:7

Remember not the sins of my youth and my rebellious ways;
according to your love remember me,
for you are good, O LORD.

*When it comes to the things of God, do we ever stop our
"youthful" transgressions or rebellious ways? Is there a time
when we are no longer feeding the dinner we don't like to the
dog or sneaking in past our curfew? It is easy, as adults, to think
that because we are living responsibly—perhaps even doing
something as significant as overcoming an addiction or caring
for a dying loved one—we aren't, in some ways, still immature
in the eyes of the Lord. How blessed are we, then, to have a God
whose boundless love deals with us patiently!*

PRAYER

Be patient with me, Lord;
my ways are not your ways—
not yet.
In your love, stay with me,
and lead me to your truth.

LIVING THE PRAYER

Today I will have one "grow up for God" moment.
What habit or tendency do I have that hinders my spiritual
maturity? Do I ever feel that I might be pushing the
boundaries of God's boundless love?

THE NEW TESTAMENT SINGS

Run from the temptations of youth, pursue righteousness, faith,
love, and peace, as one with those who call on the Lord with a
pure heart.
(2 Timothy 2:22)

PSALM 26:2

Test me, O LORD, and try me,
examine my heart and my mind.

*In the same way that we are ready to invite God into our lives
to comfort us, to tend our needs, to share our joy, or to accept
our thanks, so we should also be ready to invite God in for the
purpose of examining us and testing us, seeing if we are living
truly as people made in the divine image. We might extend the
invitation more freely if we recall that every time God enters
our lives, it is in a loving, compassionate way. To be tested or
examined by God will be a huge undertaking, but God's merciful
love for us is always greater.*

PRAYER

I welcome you, Lord!
Come to me today,
scrutinize my every thought,
word, and deed,
so that I may live in your loving-kindness.

LIVING THE PRAYER

Today I will invite God in to help me examine my life.
Do I regularly examine my day-to-day actions? Am I fearful
of what I may find, or can I acknowledge it in honesty and
humility? Does this change the way I live?

THE NEW TESTAMENT SINGS

We do not speak to please others, but to please God,
who examines our hearts.
(1 Thessalonians 2:4)

PSALM 27:5

In the day of trouble
God will keep me safe in his sanctuary,
he will hide me in the shelter of his tabernacle
and set me high upon a rock.

*We are familiar with the custom of those who have committed
some sort of transgression being able to find "sanctuary" within
the confines of a church or other building set apart for worship.
This is not because religious institutions are somehow outside
or above the law, but because "sanctuary" symbolizes what God
does for all of us. There is a safe place within God's presence for
all of us. But do we, in our daily lives, act as living symbols of
this sheltering God?*

PRAYER

I worship you, O Lord,
in your holy sanctuary.
Let me find shelter there,
and also be a haven for those
who need your protection.

LIVING THE PRAYER

*Today I will provide some sort of refuge for someone who is
troubled.*
What sorts of troubled times lead me to find shelter in God?
Do I know others who are experiencing those same kinds of
troubles? How can I help them to know some relief?

THE NEW TESTAMENT SINGS

We know that God's children do not have the habit of sinfulness,
for God's Son holds them in safety, and the evil one cannot
touch them.
(1 John 5:18)

PSALM 28:9

Save your people, Lᴏʀᴅ, and bless your inheritance;
    be their shepherd too, and hold them up forever.

*"Inheritance" in ancient Israel was a much different concept
than it is for us. An inheritance was viewed more as a future or
ongoing possession, and not so much as documenting a process
of transfer. We are not accustomed to thinking of ourselves as
God's inheritance, God's possession into the future. But that is
what we are: the way God continues to be known in the world.
This is why the psalmist asks for blessing, shepherding, and
being lifted up. But this is not something for us to be smug about
or squander. Rather it is something to be treasured and tended
with wisdom.*

PRAYER

May you find in me, O Lord,
your inheritance in the world.
Let my witness to your will
be a sign of blessing for all.

LIVING THE PRAYER

Today I will name myself God's child, and act as a child of God.
Do others see, hear, or otherwise know God's ongoing work in
the world through me? If not, what can I do to change this?

THE NEW TESTAMENT SINGS

The Holy Spirit is given as a pledge of our inheritance,
and helps us see our redemption—God's own possession—
to the praise of his glory.
(Ephesians 1:14)

PSALM 29:10
The Lord is enthroned over the vast waters;
the Lord will reign as king forever.

*Whenever the psalms put God—especially the voice of God—
in some sort of relationship to the waters or a storm, they are
evoking the essential power of God at the dawn of creation, dis-
pelling all chaos. The evangelists drew on this heritage in their
stories of Christ commanding the sea to be calm. The might of
God's voice pervades this psalm. For those familiar with Elijah
finding the voice of God not in power but in stillness (1 Kings
19:9), this might seem contradictory. But the consistency is this:
God speaks in many ways, expected and unexpected. We must
listen, to know God's presence and power everywhere.*

PRAYER

Speak, O Lord;
let me listen for you
in the wonder of life
and in the quiet moments
of every day.

LIVING THE PRAYER

*Today I will strive to listen for God's voice, so that I may be God's
voice in the world.*
How do I tend to expect God's voice to sound when I listen for
it? Powerful? Quiet? How can I broaden my listening ability?
What are the ways that I can speak with God's voice?

THE NEW TESTAMENT SINGS

For it is not you who speak, but the Spirit of your Father in
heaven speaking in you.
(Matthew 10:20)

PSALM 30:9

What gain is there for you, Lord,
in my descent to the pit?
Can the dust praise you?
Will it proclaim your faithfulness?

*The psalmist here is being a bit cheeky. This may strike some as
being irreverent toward scripture, and indeed, some modern
translations have tried to soften the questioning tone a bit. But in
taking a questioning and somewhat confrontational stance toward
the Almighty, the psalmist is acting as a true descendant of
Abraham and Moses, who did likewise. For Israel, this was another
way to prove one's intimate and personal relationship with God,
and the trust on which that relationship was founded. In a way,
thinking that God can't "take it" when we question or challenge—
like the psalmist does—actually diminishes our trust and faith in God.*

PRAYER

O God, I love you and trust your wisdom to hear me,
your mercy to stay with me,
your love to accept me as your child.

LIVING THE PRAYER

Today I will be open to questioning or challenging the ways of God.
As I seek to do God's will, are there events in my life or the world
that make me question? What are they?

THE NEW TESTAMENT SINGS

Jesus cried out with a loud voice: "Eloi, Eloi, lema sabachtani?"
which means, "My God, my God, why have you forsaken me?"
(Mark 15:34)

PSALM 31:12
I am forgotten, as though I were dead;
I am like a shard of broken pottery.

What's the big deal about broken pottery? Don't we just glue it back together or go get a replacement? In the culture of the psalmist—a culture that used, re-used, and repaired nearly everything—pottery was one of the few things that, when broken, was often irreparable. There were no adhesives, or malls to go and pick up a new piece. But even when we feel as if we are broken beyond repair, truly dead, we are not beyond the reach of the heavenly potter, who made us from clay and continues to re-make us every day.

PRAYER

Let me feel your loving hand on me,
the hand that fashioned me,
the hand that heals me,
the hand that makes me new,
today and every day, O Lord.

LIVING THE PRAYER

Today I will accept or be the healing hand of God.
When have I felt broken, beyond repair? Who around me may be feeling the same way? How can God's loving touch be present?

THE NEW TESTAMENT SINGS

A synagogue official came to Jesus and bowed down before him, saying, "My daughter has died; but lay your hand on her, and she will live."
(Matthew 9:18)

PSALM 32:5

I acknowledged my sin to you,
I did not hide my iniquity.
"I will confess my transgressions to you, LORD"
and then you forgave me all my guilt.

"Guilt" has gotten something of a bad reputation in our world. Like anything else, it can be used well or misused. Sometimes we are *guilty, and need, first off, to confess this. The confession of our transgressions to God (or to others) is what opens the door to the right relationship of forgiveness and reconciliation. Confession is good for the soul in this regard, because it opens the door that sin and guilt have shut, and lets God's healing mercy back in.*

PRAYER

Help me open my soul to you, Lord,
to acknowledge my sin,
to confess my guilt,
to restore the joy of your presence
in my life.

LIVING THE PRAYER

Today I will not rationalize away but honestly acknowledge a wrong of which I am guilty.
Do I believe and trust in God's mercy enough to allow the fullness of divine mercy and grace into my life? When forgiven, can I live joyfully, and not stay stuck in useless guilt?

THE NEW TESTAMENT SINGS

If we confess that we have sinned, God will act faithfully and righteously to forgive us, and to cleanse us from our unrighteousness.
(1 John 1:9)

PSALM 33:11

The wisdom of the Lord stands firm forever,
  the intentions of his heart through all generations.

Ancient Israel may have been a bit more comfortable than we are about believing that the intentions or will of God could be thwarted by human beings. The psalter and wisdom literature are filled with reassurances that—in spite of all evidence to the contrary—God's heart will prevail. We must hold to this belief as well, and even more importantly must be God's co-hearts, so to speak, in striving to let the world know that its firmest and truest foundation is the wisdom of the Lord.

PRAYER
....
All around me, Lord,
I see and hear and witness
a world that contradicts your wisdom.
Let me stand firm with you,
living each day with your own heart.

LIVING THE PRAYER
Today I will take some action, prompted by a news item or report, to let God's wisdom shine.

Can I refuse to be overwhelmed by the scope of today's concerns? How can I stand on the foundation of God's wisdom and, within my abilities, work for some kind of change?

THE NEW TESTAMENT SINGS

We speak God's wisdom as in a mystery, the concealed wisdom that God predestined before the ages for our glory.
(1 Corinthians 2:7)

PSALM 34:14
Turn away from evil and do good;
seek after peace, pursue it.

It is not surprising that we have so much journey/hunting imagery from a people who wandered from place to place, and who spent much of their time (even when "settled" in the Promised Land) as a nomadic tribal people. That is exactly what is going on in this verse: the turning away from a path that is wrong to walk rightly in God's ways; the searching out of peace and going after it as if it were valuable prey.

PRAYER
When I want to turn to evil ways,
turn me the right way, my Lord.
When I look for discord in my life,
help me pursue the peace
that only you can give.

LIVING THE PRAYER
Today I will "hunt down" a peaceful solution to a difficult situation.
Have I been avoiding a conflict? Do I continue stuck in unhappy or mistaken ways merely to keep from having to confront a problem? How can I turn to God and, in doing so, find a peaceful solution?

THE NEW TESTAMENT SINGS
Peace I leave with you; my peace is my gift to you.
(John 14:27)

PSALM 35:15

At my stumbling, they rejoiced;
>   my attackers rose against me when I was not aware.
They slandered me without ceasing.

It is easy to look at this psalm and its pleas for God to fight off our enemies as justification for a "God is on our side" violence, whether that violence is physical, personal, or emotional. What resonates more throughout this psalm, however, is our continual need to rely on God's strength. When we are under some form of attack, when we are being slandered, we will find our way out when we ask God to join us and help us.

PRAYER

>   When I am in trouble,
>   when I feel under attack,
>   or when others speak falsely of me,
>   I turn to you, Lord,
>   my source of strength and wisdom.

LIVING THE PRAYER

Today I will rely fully on God to help me with a troubling situation.

Do I try to work my own way out of trials, or do I call on God's help? How can I pray for God's guidance and help when others are speaking wrongly about me, and use my prayer to respond in a healthy manner?

THE NEW TESTAMENT SINGS

But I say to you who will listen: love your enemies and do good to those who hate you.
(Luke 6:27)

PSALM 36:7

How priceless is your never-ending love for us!
The mighty and the lowly find shelter
in the shadow of your wings.

Most everyone on earth is mightier than someone else, and most everyone is simultaneously lowlier as well. It is equally misguided for us to look to others for decisive protection as to think that we can provide it apart from God. The shadow cast by the wings of God is so vast and so long that it covers all of us. It also evokes the eternal love that continually soars over the world.

PRAYER

I fly to you, Lord;
be my refuge.
Soar over me as a shelter,
and let your never-ending love
rest in my heart.

LIVING THE PRAYER

Today I will grow in humility by seeking shelter in God's love. Even though God calls us to be responsible for our actions in the world, how do I keep from turning this into thinking that I'm in charge? How can I be a faithful witness, yet find a safe haven in the Lord?

THE NEW TESTAMENT SINGS

Jerusalem, Jerusalem! You kill the prophets and stone those sent to you. How I have longed to gather your children, as a hen gathers her chicks under her wings, but you would not!
(Luke 13:34)

PSALM 37:13

The LORD laughs at the wicked;
the Lord alone knows when their time
for judgment will come.

*Out of the many very human attributes the Hebrew scriptures
give the Almighty, it may be the divine laughter—especially this
all-knowing, occasional mildly scornful laughter—that is most
difficult for the modern mind to grasp. Why does God laugh at
the wicked? Why not punish them? Or end their evil ways?
Ultimately, none of us knows. As frustrating as it is to accept
this laughter as part of the divine will and wisdom, it is our only
option as people of faith.*

PRAYER

When I see evil around me,
help me to laugh your laugh
of divine wisdom.
May it strengthen me to work
against evil in my world.

LIVING THE PRAYER

Today I will try to view some evil with scorn.
What is the difference between trying to laugh away the
world's problems, and keeping them in perspective? How can
I strive to improve things for others or myself while taking
God's longer view?

THE NEW TESTAMENT SINGS

We keep our eyes fixed on Christ, author and perfecter of the faith,
who for the sake of the joy before him endured the cross, scorned
its shame, and is seated at the right hand of the throne of God.
(Hebrews 12:2)

PSALM 38:5

My wounds are foul and they fester,
because of the folly of my sin.

In ancient Israel, religious and health codes and their beliefs were
tightly bound together. A visible sore was cause for concern in
the whole community, especially if it looked leprous. Disease and
its symptoms were viewed as punishment, caused by individual
or communal sin. For the psalmist to talk about foul, festering
sores caused by the folly of sin is a very serious statement. These
connections may not necessarily be part of a more contemporary
way of believing, but illness is still part of human frailty, and can
in some instances be caused by the folly of sin. Visible or not, the
wounds of sin afflict us all.

PRAYER

God who is my life and health,
keep me from the folly of sin.
Heal the wounds
that my transgressions have caused me or others.

LIVING THE PRAYER

Today I will allow God's healing touch into my life or the lives
of others.
In what ways has the folly of my sin wounded me or others?
How is my life or the life of those around me less healthy
because of it?

THE NEW TESTAMENT SINGS

Confess your sins to one another; pray for each other so you may
be healed. For the prayer of the righteous is potent and effective.
(James 5:16)

PSALM 39:3

My heart was growing hot within me,
I meditated and the fire burned;
finally my tongue had to speak.

In this psalm, the psalmist speaks of "holy heartburn" in the context of keeping silent in order not to say anything sinful or wrong while surrounded by enemies. When enough is enough, the psalmist's tongue speaks to implore God to explain fully the troublesome situation and the futility of trying to be faithful. It is a consistent scriptural theme that we cannot, ultimately, keep silent when we are afraid, confused, wondering how or if God is present. A certain heating of the heart—a sign of God with us— usually impels us onward.

PRAYER

Dwell in my heart, O Lord;
set it on fire, loosen my tongue.
Let me always be true
and honest in my love for you.

LIVING THE PRAYER

Today I will openly express some doubt, fear, or challenge that has been kept in my heart.
Can I truly feel God's presence in the troubled stirrings of my heart? How much do I trust my expression of the feelings I've kept trapped there?

THE NEW TESTAMENT SINGS

They said, "Were not our hearts burning within us as he spoke to us on the way, explaining the scriptures to us?"
(Luke 24:32)

PSALM 40:5

O Lord my God, many are your wondrous deeds.
What you have in store for us
no one can possibly tell;
if I tried to tell them all,
they would be too many for me.

There is a happy domino effect when we reflect on the wonders of God's love. As we remember or think about one, it leads to another, which leads to one or two others, which continues to lead us onward in a litany of blessings. Though doing this might seem like a useless exercise to the more practically-minded, allowing ourselves to be immersed in God's marvels can be a great boost for our personal faith and hope for the future, and can inspire us to continue living as witnesses to the glory of God.

PRAYER
....

I love you, my Lord!
You have filled the world
with the bounty of your miracles;
I praise you for the splendor
of your works!

LIVING THE PRAYER

Today I will set aside some time to name some of God's glorious actions in the world.
How long can I sustain my praise when I think of God's many blessings? How does this time span contrast with God's eternal love?

THE NEW TESTAMENT SINGS

Blessed be the God and Father of our Lord Jesus Christ, who has bestowed on us every spiritual blessing of heaven in Christ. (Ephesians 1:3)

PSALM 41:13
Praise to the Lord, the God of Israel,
from everlasting to everlasting.
Amen, and Amen.

*It is not typical for the psalms to conclude with a formal prayer
ending that expresses God's eternal nature and the "so be it"
of an Amen. Some scholars have concluded that this does not
mean the psalms didn't have formalized conclusions in
worship, only that the Israelites knew how to do this without
it being written down. An ending like this can be a signal from
the psalmist that we need to stop taking any part of our prayer
for granted. Whether it is naming God at the beginning,
or affirming our faith in God at the end, sometimes we have to
pray it all out loud.*

PRAYER

Almighty and ever-living God,
your kindness and faithfulness
are as eternal as your love for us.
This I believe; to you I pray. Amen.

LIVING THE PRAYER

Today I will pray to God, taking nothing for granted.
God certainly knows when I am praying, so what benefit is
there to a stricter form for my prayer? Can I use a variety of
prayer styles to deepen my spiritual life?

THE NEW TESTAMENT SINGS

I will pray with the spirit and with the mind also; I will sing
with the spirit and with the mind as well.
(1 Corinthians 14:15)

PSALM 42:5

Why do you despair, my soul?
Why are you disturbed in me?
Hope in God, once again I will praise him
for the help of his presence.

The psalmist sets up an interesting conversation between the individual praying the psalm and the prayer's soul as a separate persona (perhaps easier for the psalmist's imagination than for our modern one), with the divine presence as a third party or outside force. The whole psalm fluctuates between addressing the Almighty and the individual's soul. This sort of fluidity can be beneficial to any prayer life, whether we are seeking some sort of comfort in time of despair, or wanting to reflect more deeply on the workings of our own soul.

PRAYER

Hear my soul
as it cries out to you, O Lord.
O my soul,
offer your whole being to God,
your joy and salvation!

LIVING THE PRAYER

Today I will become more aware of the life of my soul.
Am I fully attentive to my soul's various states, whether it is grieving or rejoicing? Can I think of my soul expressing these things, or is "me" the only way I do this?

THE NEW TESTAMENT SINGS

Jesus then said to them, "My soul is deeply grieved, to the point of death; remain here and keep watch with me."
(Matthew 26:38)

PSALM 43:1

Vindicate me, my God!
> Plead my case against an ungodly nation.
> Deliver me from the deceitful and unjust!

There may be no more difficult times to live God's covenant faithfully than those times when we are called upon to stand up to or go against the ways of the society around us. The psalmists were never ones to let the Almighty off easily in these tough times. If acting righteously is the will of God, then God also needs to stand against ungodly behavior, dishonest practices, and the injustices of the world. This psalm casts the scene in a courtroom, with God as an advocate, sort of a defense attorney. We, too, can remember that God indeed is on our side and will always plead our cause.

PRAYER

Send your Spirit, O Lord,
as my advocate
to help me do your will
when the world wants me
to follow its own ways.

LIVING THE PRAYER

Today I will, with God's help, stand up for what is right.
Do I allow my inaction or silence to pass as not cooperating with sinfulness? Am I afraid to speak up because I don't truly believe that God stands with me?

THE NEW TESTAMENT SINGS

I will pray to the Father, who will give you another Advocate, who will dwell with you forever.
(John 14:16)

PSALM 44:12

You, LORD, sold your people for a mere pittance;
you made no profit from selling them.

The central event and metaphor of Israel's faith was God's
deliverance of them from their slavery in Egypt. Here the
psalmist describes a God so disgusted with the Chosen People's
faithlessness that they are re-sold into slavery. An extra level of
insult is added when the Lord doesn't even make a profit,
but merely wants to be rid of them as quickly as possible.
In a world that knew slavery, the only reason to own slaves was
to accomplish quality work, and the reason to sell them was
for profit. By violating their covenant, Israel evidently provided
neither reason.

PRAYER

Keep me faithful to you,
O Lord my God.
Do not let me be enslaved by the world,
but hold me as your chosen child.

LIVING THE PRAYER

Today I will refuse to be enslaved by something contrary to
God's will.
How does my faithlessness help me remain in bondage
to whatever is not good or true? Though God loves me
unconditionally, what do I do that still causes pain?

THE NEW TESTAMENT SINGS

It is for freedom that Christ liberated us. Stand secure, and do not
allow yourselves to be burdened again with the bonds of slavery.
(Galatians 5:1)

PSALM 45:7

You, my king, love righteousness and hate wickedness;
therefore your God has set you above others,
anointing you with the oil of gladness.

*The king in this psalm is Israel's king, it's not a metaphor for God,
though the line "you love righteousness and hate wickedness"
sounds like a description of the Almighty. The expectation here
is that the one anointed (in Hebrew, Messiah) will be the living
image of the Lord. Too often in our faith history we have made
God more king-like (God resembling earthly rulers) and
diminished our expectations that our leaders will act more
God-like. But before we breathe a sigh of relief that this isn't
expected of us, we need to recall that all of us are made in God's
image.*

PRAYER

You anointed me
for your service, my God.
Created in your image,
let me love what you love,
and live as you live.

LIVING THE PRAYER

Today I will be God's image in the world.
Are my daily thoughts, words, and deeds godly? Can others
see a loving, kind, merciful, and faithful God in the way
I live my life?

THE NEW TESTAMENT SINGS

Christ is the image of the unseen God, the firstborn of the whole
creation.
(Colossians 1:15)

PSALM 46:10

Be still, know that I alone am God;
I will be exalted in every nation,
throughout the earth.

How busy we can get, being faithful messengers of God's will in the world; how easy for us to despair at the overwhelming task presented to us! The danger that we all encounter is thinking or believing that it is our work we are doing, not God's. But the contrary danger is to be inactive, to do nothing. What the psalmist tells us here is that every now and then we need to slow down or calm down to remember that it is truly God's will for which we are striving, and that—ultimately—it is God, and not we, who will be glorified by the fulfillment of heaven's reign in our midst.

PRAYER

May you be exalted, O God,
in the stillness of my heart,
in the witness of my deeds,
in every time and every place.

LIVING THE PRAYER

Today I will set aside some time of stillness to be re-energized for a faithful life.
Am I able to distinguish between sinful inaction and grace-filled stillness? How can my quiet reflection and active discipleship both exalt the Lord?

THE NEW TESTAMENT SINGS

Christ is the high priest we require: one who is holy, blameless, undefiled, apart from sinners, and exalted above the heavens. (Hebrews 7:26)

PSALM 47:9

The rulers of the nations come together
as the people of the God of Abraham,
the earth's rulers belong to God;
let God be greatly exalted.

This is a rather remarkable statement from the people of Israel during the time of their monarchy, when there was a rather closed/bloodline/tribal understanding of how God's covenant was shared. To include all the rulers of the enemy pagan nations among those named as Abraham's descendants could have been viewed as both faithless and unpatriotic. Yet this conclusion of the psalm tells us that God's greatness is so incomprehensible that even those whom our limited human view places outside God's promises are included. As always, Israel's reaction to God's greatness is great exaltation.

PRAYER

How great and glorious
is your love for all people,
Lord of the nations.
Help me grow in your love
and share it more generously.

LIVING THE PRAYER

Today I will try to broaden my horizon of who is included among God's chosen children.

Are there individuals or groups whom I sometimes think of as being out of God's reach? How can I improve my own reaching out to them?

THE NEW TESTAMENT SINGS

And if you belong to Christ, you are a descendant of Abraham, an heir according to the promise.
(Galatians 3:29)

PSALM 48:9

Inside the walls of our temple, O God,
we meditate on your unfailing love.

The paradox of this verse isn't immediately apparent: we meditate on what is unfailing within what does fail . . . the walls of temples built by human hands and our own mortal flesh. This doesn't mean that we don't utilize sacred spaces or our own physical bodies to mediate, pray, and offer worship; but even these things can become idols. The most ancient or glorious of religious places are nothing compared to God. The same can be said of the most eloquent preacher or gifted musician. Instead, all of these gifts from God remind us only of what truly lasts: the infinite presence and eternal love of the God whom we worship.

PRAYER

In the beauty of your holiness
I offer my prayer and worship
to you, Lord.
Let me dwell on what truly lasts,
and come to dwell with you forever.

LIVING THE PRAYER

Today I will use something or someplace impermanent to reflect on or pray about God's eternal love.
Are there particular times or places that I feel are better suited to my praise of God? How can I broaden my understanding?

THE NEW TESTAMENT SINGS

In Christ God's whole household is built up together, rising to become a holy temple in the Lord.
(Ephesians 2:21)

PSALM 49:20
Those who have riches,
but lack understanding,
are like the beasts, doomed to die.

*This is not a surprising statement, and is characteristic of
the larger genre of Israel's literature known as the "wisdom"
literature. The example of Solomon, patron of this literature
(he who preferred wisdom to power, fame, or riches) echoes
here strongly. Israel's wisdom literature doesn't usually condemn
wealth or power or renown. What it does condemn is thinking
that these things, in and of themselves, are signs of God's favor.
The truest sign of God's favor is having the understanding to
use these gifts as wise stewards, to further God's commands and
covenant in the world. As we look at our own resources, we can
similarly scrutinize ourselves to discern if we truly use them in
wisdom.*

PRAYER
God of all insight and understanding,
I thank you for every gift.
Make me a wise and generous steward of them,
for your honor and glory alone.

LIVING THE PRAYER

*Today I will use some gift or resource wisely, as a sign of God's
providence for others.*
What resources do I have that I sometimes use selfishly?
How can I reform my life so that I use them wisely, selflessly?

THE NEW TESTAMENT SINGS

How deep are the riches of the wisdom and knowledge of God!
(Romans 11:33)

PSALM 50:12

If I, your LORD, were hungry, I would not need to tell you,
for all the world is mine, and everything in it.

*The Almighty is being a bit of a smart aleck here, making fun
of some of Israel's neighbors who stuffed food sacrifices into the
mouths of the statues of their deities. Since Israel had a strict
prohibition against any sort of visual representation of their
God, this was not a practice they would follow, but they are
being warned here against thinking that mere fulfillment of
religious ritual (including their own forms of sacrifices) acted
as some sort of way to control heaven. This is a danger we still
fall into today, and a warning we would do well to heed.*

PRAYER

I offer you a sacrifice
of thanks and praise,
of my life lived according to your will,
my God, maker of heaven and earth.

LIVING THE PRAYER

Today I will take one of my religious practices off auto-pilot.
What do I do daily to give thanks and praise to God? Has it
become rote? Do I think it will make God act a certain way?

THE NEW TESTAMENT SINGS

To love the Lord your God with all your heart, understanding,
and strength, and to love others as yourself is more valuable
than all your burnt offerings or sacrifices.
(Mark 12:33)

PSALM 51:4

Against you alone, Lord, have I sinned,
   I have done what is evil in your sight;
so you shall be proven right when you speak against me,
   justified when you judge.

*This psalm is rather famously connected with David's
repentance after his infidelity with Bathsheba and murder of
her husband, Uriah. It could seem odd that David would say
he sinned only against God. This is not to say he did not wrong
Bathsheba or Uriah, or abuse the power God gave him, but it
says that God is so very deeply and intimately connected with
those who have had sins committed against them that it is,
indeed, like sinning against God. This is what renders God's
judgments (against David or against us) true and righteous.*

PRAYER

Your boundless love, O Lord,
is in everything, every place,
in every person I sin against.
Help me see your face everywhere,
so I might sin no more.

LIVING THE PRAYER

*Today I will seek God's pardon by asking forgiveness from
someone I have sinned against.*
Do I think it merely enough to confess my sin to God?
Can I see God's love in those whom I have wronged?

THE NEW TESTAMENT SINGS

Peter said: "So repent, and turn to God so your sins will be wiped
away, and a time of refreshment will come from the Lord."
(Acts 3:19–20)

PSALM 52:1

Why boast of your evil, O mighty ones?
For the steadfast love of God endures forever.

It would seem that the world of the insecure need to claim petty victories, to gloat, to relish the disadvantage at which we've placed others is not a world unknown to the psalmist. The opening of this psalm is a reply to a snitch who betrayed David to his enemy Saul. Rather than delighting in the advantage, we hear that these small human machinations are evil, and not what God desires. It is easy enough, in our own little skirmishes that we blow out of proportion, to behave this very same way, and not like those who truly live in the light of a God who is steadfast and loving.

PRAYER

Help me live in your love,
my faithful God!
Let me treat others rightly,
not seeking my own gain,
but your merciful ways.

LIVING THE PRAYER

Today I will end a little squabble that I've turned into a major battle.
Do I feel a need to be victorious all the time? Am I willing to do anything to achieve this end, even if it is evil?

THE NEW TESTAMENT SINGS

These godless ones always grumble and find fault; they follow their own evil desires, boasting of themselves, flattering others for their own advantage.
(Jude 1:16)

PSALM 53:2

God looks down from the heavens,
looks upon all humanity;
looking to see if anyone is truly wise,
if anyone is seeking God.

The theme of God scrutinizing the earth to find even a few faithful people is a common one in Israel's scriptures. The accounts of Noah before the flood and Abraham in Sodom both contain this theme. Here God is setting the standard pretty low, not even looking for faithful and observant followers, but trying to discover if anyone is even merely seeking God's ways. God doesn't just look among those who might be expected to be seekers of wisdom, but looks on all humanity, looking among all those created in the divine image. What we need to do each day, in order to be living in wisdom, is to seek God.

PRAYER

I need you and I seek you,
my loving God.
May you find in me
a faithful one
who searches for your wisdom.

LIVING THE PRAYER

Today I will be the "seeker" whom God is looking for.
Do I get inactively content, even smug, that I am always in God's presence? How do I need to continue my seeking or questing for God's wisdom?

THE NEW TESTAMENT SINGS

Live wisely among those who do not believe, making the most of every opportunity.
(Colossians 4:5)

PSALM 54:6

I offer you a voluntary sacrifice;
>   I will praise the goodness of your name, O Lord.

As Israel's worship grew more formalized around the temple, so did its code of prescribed sacrifices. For the average citizen, there wasn't much to spare from everyday life, which made tithing regular offerings a sign of their dedication to the covenant. An extra, voluntary offering really meant something. When we talk about "sacrificing" today, we can use it as a code for surrendering what we don't truly need anyway (the daily candy from the snack machine). How much more meaningful would a voluntary sacrifice be, given from where it hurts!

PRAYER
....
In the goodness
and bounty of your love,
hear my prayer, O Lord.
Increase my generosity;
make me ready to offer myself for you.

LIVING THE PRAYER

Today I will sacrifice something truly significant.
Do I give to the needy or charitable causes only out of my excess? Am I willing to endure real self-denial to improve the lives of others?

THE NEW TESTAMENT SINGS

Jesus called his disciples to him, saying: "Truly, I tell you that poor widow's two coins in the treasury are more than all the others." (Mark 12:43)

PSALM 55:6

Oh that I had the wings of a dove,
so I could fly away, and at last find rest.

*This very well may be one of the most poignant expressions
in all of the psalmists' laments. All of us, like this particular
psalmist, know the feeling of being surrounded by troubles and
questions and worries. Thinking we can escape them all, we
pray to God to carry us far away from them. How often, in these
situations, do we find that God instead may give us wings to fly
directly into the very situations we want to escape? The miracle
is not God's giving us wings to fly away, but giving us strength to
encounter, endure, and thereby find our true rest.*

PRAYER

I fly to you, O Lord,
for only you can sustain me,
strengthen me, support me
in times of trouble.
In you alone I find my rest.

LIVING THE PRAYER

*Today, with God's strength, I will face a significant worry in
my life.*
Are there things going on in my life that I consistently fly
away from? Does this truly resolve them and allow me to rest?
How might dealing with them be better for me?

THE NEW TESTAMENT SINGS

The Lord knows how to rescue the godly from their times of
trial, and keeps the wicked under chastisement until their
lasting judgment.
(2 Peter 2:9)

PSALM 56:8

Record my sorrows, LORD;
>　put my tears in your wineskin,
>　have you no record of them?

*The image of God placing our tears into a wineskin, into a
vessel from which one drinks, is extremely intimate. It
profoundly expresses God's deep awareness of and involvement
in our sorrow, a sorrow that God not only keeps, but drinks
from. And yet, in characteristic fashion, the psalmist includes
(as a reminder, perhaps) a question to make sure God is
tending to this matter. It is not so much an expression of doubt
as a way to remind God of the faithfulness and love promised in
the covenant made and renewed with the people of Israel,
God's chosen ones.*

PRAYER

In times of sorrow,
I know you are with me,
God of faithfulness.
In your great love, hear my grieving;
pay heed to my tears.

LIVING THE PRAYER

*Today I will recall when I wept, and I will think of God keeping
my tears.*
When I have been mournful, have I turned to God only to
solve or ease my troubles? Do I allow God into my sorrow
fully, to share its burden with me?

THE NEW TESTAMENT SINGS

"My soul is overwhelmed with sorrow to the point of death,"
Jesus said. "Stay here, keep watch."
(Mark 14:34)

PSALM 57:4

I dwell in the midst of lions;
I lie amid hungry beasts,
those whose teeth are spears and arrows,
whose tongues are sharp swords.

Even the most urban of Israel's people did not live all that far from herds and flocks and the carnivorous predators they attracted. Even in the city people kept livestock and, with them, the threat of attack from various predators. The psalmist's first audience was not thinking of the Wizard of Oz's "lions and tigers and bears," but of real beasts as the image of people who were armed, even if only with sharpened tongues. Most of us today have to work harder to make these images come to life, but God's faithful servants can still dwell in this kind of danger.

PRAYER

Eternal God, let me be vigilant,
always aware and watchful
for that which will harm me
when I try to live as your faithful servant.

LIVING THE PRAYER

Today I will hunt for "beasts" in my own world that seek to harm me.
Without becoming paranoid, can I look at my life and see the people or values that are hurtful? Do I keep my own sharp tongue at the ready to injure others?

THE NEW TESTAMENT SINGS

With our tongue we praise our Lord and Father, with the same tongue we curse others, made in the image of God. (James 3:9)

PSALM 58:4

The wicked spit venom like deadly snakes;
>   they are like deaf cobras, their ears stopped up.

This is one of the most colorful animal images in the psalms.
It goes on to describe how these deaf cobras cannot be charmed,
no matter how skillful a musician the charmer may be.
How novel for us to think of God's word and wisdom as
being the snake charmer's tune that keeps the wicked
(including us!) from striking with their poisonous fangs.
Perhaps today we might think of the cobra's ears being blocked
up with headphones, or merely being so over-bombarded with
an array of aural (and visual) stimulation that God's charming
music just can't make it through.

PRAYER

Make music for me, Lord God,
of your love and truth.
Let my ears be opened
and my life kept from wickedness.

LIVING THE PRAYER

Today I will turn off one source of noise that deafens me to
God's voice.
Am I constantly filling my life with sounds of different sorts?
Even if not, what deafens me or distracts me from
the beautiful song of God's grace?

THE NEW TESTAMENT SINGS

The hearts of these people are hardened; their ears cannot hear,
they have closed their eyes so they cannot see, and their hearts
cannot understand, so they cannot come to me so I may heal them.
(Acts 28:27)

PSALM 59:11

Do not slay your enemies, Lord,
>or my people will forget;
>>but scatter them by your power, bring them down,
>>O Lord, our shield.

"Keep your friends close and your enemies closer" goes the proverb. There's a bit of that at work here; the psalmist (echoing others) acknowledges Israel's tendency to have a short attention span when it comes to God's mighty deeds or saving power on their behalf. Enemies that were scattered (not a threat or nuisance) but still alive—and still Israel's enemies—could serve as an effective reminder that the need for God's salvation was always a reality. There are forces, values, and persons in our own lives who, in their negative way, can also help keep us close to God.

PRAYER
....
>You are my safety
>and my shield, O Lord.
>Help me recall the wonder of
>your saving power in my life.

LIVING THE PRAYER

Today I will recall a time when God saved me.
What are some of the "enemies" that try to keep me from living faithfully? How has God scattered them in the past? In gratitude, can I turn to God to keep them from my life?

THE NEW TESTAMENT SINGS

Be alert and look for your enemy, the devil, who prowls like a lion, looking for someone to devour.
(1 Peter 5:8)

PSALM 60:3

You have given your people hardships;
given us wine that makes us reel.

*Wine-making was not as exact an art or as highly-regulated
in ancient times as it is today. Fermentation could vary wildly
(making one wine weak and another incredibly potent, even
wine served at the same event), or it could go sour faster than
expected in the heat and sun or when improperly stored.
But one would expect only choice and flavorful wine from God!
(Isaiah the prophet said so.) When the foul wine is given by
God's hand, it is a slap in the face that sends us reeling.
This psalm, written in the midst of war and strife in Israel,
thinks that God has offered such wine.*

PRAYER

When I enter times
of trouble or hardship,
stay with me, Lord.
Help me endure my trial
to be more fully devoted to you.

LIVING THE PRAYER

*Today I will embrace a hardship or shortcoming or trial as a way
that God helps me to grow.*
Are there things in my life that I think are hardships? Which
of these might actually be a gift from God to help me grow in
grace?

THE NEW TESTAMENT SINGS

"We must endure many hardships, so we might enter the kingdom
of God," Paul and Barnabas told the disciples.
(Acts 14:22)

PSALM 61:2

From the ends of the earth I cry out for help, LORD,
when my heart feels faint;
lead me to a towering rock of refuge.

*Israel's connection to a geographic place—the Promised Land—
had spiritual implications. This was true of Jerusalem, built
high on a fortified hill. This prayer, however, is being cried
out from a distant, not-promised place. A place so far away,
perhaps, that the journey there (and away from God) has made
the pray-er faint. But the expression of faith is still strong.
In our own lives we can sometimes feel that we are in a safe
place, yet suddenly discover that it is a troubled place instead,
perhaps because we have unknowingly (or by deceiving
ourselves) gone far away from God. But no place is so far
away that God cannot hear our pleas.*

PRAYER

Even when I feel far from you,
I know you are near, Lord.
Bring me from all barren places
into the promise of your love.

LIVING THE PRAYER

*Today I will look at my spiritual "road map" to see if I am distant
from God.*
What do I consider my "safe" spiritual places? Is there a
possibility that, even in these places, I can distance myself
from God?

THE NEW TESTAMENT SINGS

Those of us who have fled to God for refuge are confident;
we cling fast to the hope that lies before us.
(Hebrews 6:18)

PSALM 62:9

The lowly born are worthless as the wind,
the powerful are a lie.
Weigh them both on a scale,
they are lighter than a breath.

From the beginning, it seems that God has destined human beings to be fulfilled in other human beings; the Genesis creation accounts narrate this, and Abraham's promise is made in terms of numerous descendants. It seems curious here, then, that we are told to trust in no other human beings, even though they are made in the image and likeness of God. We are being cautioned, of course, not to turn other mere mortals into false gods, but to turn with them as one to place our trust in God alone.

PRAYER

You have given me the blessing
of family, friends, neighbors,
God, my Creator.
Help me find your image in them,
so that we may all live to serve you.

LIVING THE PRAYER

Today I will join with at least one other person—lowly or powerful—in honoring God alone.
What is the difference between finding God's presence in others and making them into little gods? Am I able to see God's grace in them, but also know their shortcomings, along with my own?

THE NEW TESTAMENT SINGS

Wherever two or three have gathered together in my name,
I am present in their midst.
(Matthew 18:20)

PSALM 63:5
You have filled my soul as at a banquet,
my mouth sings your praises with joy.

It was one thing for the people of Israel to understand God's bounty for their bodies—good harvests, healthy crops, plentiful rains—as a blessing; in a world where food and water often were in short supply, these truly were signs of a generous God. But God isn't merely bountiful in supplying our bodies with what they need; our very souls, our spirits, are filled with the riches of heaven. We are not merely sustained by the hand of the Lord, but we are fulfilled as well. What else is there to do but sing with joy!

PRAYER

I sing with joy to you,
generous and gracious God;
you continue to care for me
in my body, in my mind, and in my spirit.

LIVING THE PRAYER

Today I will take the moment of a hunger pang to remind myself of the banquet that God gives my soul.
Can I allow the hungers that I experience to put me back in touch with my spiritual life? Do I ever fast to energize my prayer life and my acts of charity?

THE NEW TESTAMENT SINGS

Jesus said: "Do not worry about these things, saying 'What shall we eat? What shall we drink? What will we wear?' "
(Matthew 6:31)

PSALM 64:6

As the wicked plot injustices, they say,
"We have the perfect plan!"
How cunning are the human heart and mind.

One of the classic literary ways to refer to the loss of the Garden of Eden is as the loss of innocence. This has a ring of truth to it, for it often seems that the amazing capacities and energies of the human heart and mind are put to their fullest use in the crafting of injustices, rather than in the promotion of what is right, just, and peaceful. It is odd that we attach words like "perfect" to our plans that are intended to be wicked or unjust, or seek to harm others.

PRAYER

You have made me in your image,
Lord of life and light.
Let me use every energy and talent
to bring your justice and joy
to the world around me.

LIVING THE PRAYER

Today I will use my intelligence and imagination to do some good in the world.
Do I devote my energies to any sort of unjust or unfair plots? How can re-directing that energy, even on a small scale, be of benefit to me and to others?

THE NEW TESTAMENT SINGS

When we come to unity, we will no longer be infantile, tossed and blown around by the wind of every new teaching, by the cunning and craftiness of deceitful schemes.
(Ephesians 4:14)

PSALM 65:11

You crown the year with your plenty, LORD,
every pathway overflows with abundance.

In a place like a tropical rainforest, a path will soon grow over with the abundant life there. In a place like Israel, where even the most verdant areas were precariously dependent on water, paths pretty much remained paths: hard, dry, dusty, or muddy, ready for trekking, with only the occasional sprig of green taking root before getting trampled. How abundant must God's crown of goodness be, to make even these hard, dry, trodden-down places grow abundantly! Are we able to live in a God-like manner, and bring some plenty to those whose lives have hard pathways in them?

PRAYER

Your abundant goodness
is the crown of my life, my Lord!
Let me selflessly share it
with those who find the way of life hard.

LIVING THE PRAYER

Today I will soften the hard path that another person is walking. Can I express my thankfulness for God's goodness by sharing it with others? How can I encourage others to do the same?

THE NEW TESTAMENT SINGS

For when you have plenty, you can help those who are in need. When they, in turn, have plenty, they may share with you in your need.
(2 Corinthians 8:14)

PSALM 66:14

I will fulfill those vows my lips promised,
which my mouth spoke when I was in trouble.

We've all seen it: the scene of the nowhere-else-to-turn
individuals who, for the first time in a long time, drop to their
knees to re-establish contact with heaven and make fervent
promises of reform, if only God will get them out of trouble.
Even if we're people who drop to our knees in prayer regularly,
there's a good chance that the things we promise God only get
promised because we're in trouble. It's much better for us if we
offer vows or promises when we're prompted, like God, to make
our promises out of love (as in marriage). And when we live day
by day in that love, those promises are much easier to keep.

PRAYER

In your great love, O God,
you have promised your
love, faithfulness, and mercy;
let me, in love,
return the promise to you.

LIVING THE PRAYER

Today I will live out the covenant promise of faithfulness made
between God and me.
What are some of the basic daily actions of those who love
others? Do I, at the very least, say "I love you" to God each
day?

THE NEW TESTAMENT SINGS

Listen, then: Has not God chosen those who are poor in the eyes of
the world to be rich in faith; has God not promised the inheritance
of the kingdom to those who love him?
(James 2:5)

PSALM 67:3

Let the peoples praise you, O God;
let all the peoples praise you.

*This refrain recurs twice in this brief psalm, a psalm that
describes God's just guidance and generous blessing of the whole
earth. In the psalm, as in our lives, God's praise is the way that
our lives respond to and are oriented toward God's presence in
the world. The whole book of psalms, in fact, is known as
the* tehillim *(praises), since praising God is what always
undergirds our lives. We sometimes give thanks (which is
different from praising), we sometimes lament, we sometimes
bless, we sometimes question or challenge, we sometimes
receive or offer wisdom, but we always give God our praise.*

PRAYER

In the midst of my joys and blessings,
in my times of sorrow or doubt,
I give you my praise, O Lord,
a sign of my love for you.

LIVING THE PRAYER

Today I will choose an "unexpected" time to offer praise to God.
When have I been saddest, most doubtful, or perhaps
even angry with God? Did I still offer my praise? Do I also
remember to praise God during the good times?

THE NEW TESTAMENT SINGS

Jesus, in the joy of the Spirit, said "I praise you, Father, Lord of
heaven and earth, for you have hidden things from the learned
and wise, yet revealed them to little children."
(Luke 10:21)

PSALM 68:6

God gives the lonely a family,
and leads forth prisoners to freedom with singing;
but the rebellious are brought to live
in a sun-scorched land.

*The Hebrew scriptures don't have what our modern minds
conceive of as a fire-filled hell, but they were familiar with fire
and heat as signs of divine judgment. Earlier on, this psalm
speaks of God's enemies vanishing like smoke or melting like
wax. An even harsher judgment is that of being left alive, but to
live in a land scorched by the sun's fire, unable to provide water
to quench thirst or food to quell hunger. Here, too, is the "upside
down" God at work, taking care of those who have no family
household (often by abandonment or shunning) and criminals
who not only are freed, but sing with God's joy!*

PRAYER

Help me remain loyal to you,
God of justice.
Let me be a sign
of your tender mercy
on those cast aside by the world.

LIVING THE PRAYER

Today I will seek God's loving presence where I least expect to find it.
Do I sometimes think I know who's "in" and who's "out" in
God's plan? Am I willing to allow my expectations to be upset
by God's grace?

THE NEW TESTAMENT SINGS

They will never be hungry or thirsty again; nor will they be
scorched by the heat of the sun.
(Revelation 7:16)

PSALM 69:2

I have sunk into deep mire,
I have no foothold;
I am in the deep waters
and a flood overpowers me.

It is a scary feeling to have been, one moment, in a safe and manageable depth of the ocean, and then suddenly to find yourself just a bit further out, in a place where a current has carried you past a reachable bottom foothold. But we're the ones who wade out toward the deep waters to begin with. This psalm tells us that we do a similar thing to ourselves in our spiritual lives, wading out, thinking we can manage it a bit deeper and a bit deeper, until we have gotten ourselves to a point of being overpowered. This is the point at which we usually cry out for God's help.

PRAYER

I know you will rescue me
in times of distress, my Savior.
Give me the wisdom to stay away
from that which will harm me,
so I need only cry out to you in praise.

LIVING THE PRAYER

Today I will stop wading out into dangerous depths that I cannot manage.
What unhealthy behavior might have I just begun? Do I think "just a little deeper" is safe? How deep into it will I have to be to cry out for help?

THE NEW TESTAMENT SINGS

When Peter saw the wind and waves, he was frightened and started to sink. "Lord, save me!" he cried.
(Matthew 14:30)

PSALM 70:4

May all who seek you, LORD,
be filled with joy and gladness.
May those who love your salvation
cry out "Let God be exalted!"

*Seeking or searching for God's salvation, or to live in God's
ways, is an activity that the psalms find extremely praiseworthy.
Even those who seek the Lord are worthy of being filled with joy
and gladness. One doesn't have to successfully find the Lord's
presence; the quest alone can be a source of joy. The same sense
applies to loving God's saving power itself: when we know this
love, it is so great that we cannot keep silent about it, but must
shout out our exaltation of our great and loving God.*

PRAYER

My life overflows
with love and gladness and joy,
for I strive to seek your face, O Lord,
and I know your saving power each day.

LIVING THE PRAYER

*Today I will be aware of the happiness that my pursuit of God's
will brings me.*
Do I think that being faithful and obedient to the Lord's
ways is a burden? How can I find, and express, true joy and
gladness in growing in grace day by day?

THE NEW TESTAMENT SINGS

I will return to restore the house of David. Its ruins will I rebuild
and restore, so all people might seek the Lord.
(Acts 15:16)

PSALM 71:18

Even when I am old and gray,
O God, do not abandon me,
but let me declare your might to a new generation,
your power to those yet to come.

*There is an understandable tendency in our times for the Church
to do whatever it can to attract and retain young members.
It is assumed that older people remember their faith, but
younger people necessarily do not, and the evidence is there
to support this assumption. But just as the psalmist here prays
not to be abandoned, communities that give witness to God's
presence cannot abandon the old and gray, nor reject the
things of faith that they inherited, treasured, enriched, and
hand on to a new generation. As God looks on every age in love,
so must we, remembering to see as God sees.*

PRAYER

I know you have numbered my every hair,
God who gives me life.
Let me, in every one of my ages,
sing your name into the days to come.

LIVING THE PRAYER

*Today I will hand on the faith to someone younger, or learn my
faith from someone older.*
Am I caught up in the latest fads in my religion? When it
comes to "tradition" do I get overly protective?

THE NEW TESTAMENT SINGS

To God be the glory in the church, and in Christ Jesus our Lord,
to all generations to come, forever and ever. Amen.
(Ephesians 3:21)

PSALM 72:18

Praise the LORD, the God of Israel,
who alone does these marvelous deeds.

*This is a case of "the last shall be first" in scripture. It is
possible to read the opening verse (a prayer that God will
endow the king with justice and righteousness) and then this
closing verse, and truly have a sense of the whole psalm,
a litany praising the king's advocacy for the poor, weak, and
lowly, and the subsequent reward: the tribute of nations, a name
that will endure for generations. It's our tendency to think of
these final words, then, as insignificant, but they unlock the
whole thing with one of the psalter's favorite themes: God's
praise comes first, for it is truly God alone who does these
wondrous things!*

PRAYER

You love righteousness, my Lord God,
and you do wondrous things.
Make my life a source of your justice,
so all may come to give you praise.

LIVING THE PRAYER

*Today I will act on behalf of the poor or weak, not to improve
my reputation, but to praise God.*
How selfless can I be when I act justly and charitably?
When others praise me, can I turn the praise toward God?

THE NEW TESTAMENT SINGS

For God has chosen those despised by the world, counted as
nothing, and used them to bring to nothing what the world
treasures.
(1 Corinthians 1:28)

PSALM 73:4

For the arrogant have no struggles,
their bodies are healthy and well-fed.

*Like this psalmist, most of us have been envious of those who
seem to be living the good life and enjoying success upon
success, even though we know they are arrogant and wicked,
not walking in the ways desired by God. We covet the lives
they lead, at least the exterior of their lives that we can see.
Sometimes we cave in and begin to imitate them ourselves,
and it is then that we can start to discover that leading a life
contrary to God's will can get very complex, filled with
struggles, and that well-fed bodies aren't necessarily healthy.
Better for us to turn away from the snare of envy right away.*

PRAYER

Keep my life simple and obedient,
in your great love, my Lord.
Do not let me be jealous of others,
but be satisfied to walk humbly with you.

LIVING THE PRAYER

Today I will stop one jealousy that leads me away from God.
What "success" of somebody else do I envy, even though I
know it would harm me spiritually? Can I truly be satisfied
living a godly life?

THE NEW TESTAMENT SINGS

You are still living sinfully, jealous of each other and quarreling.
This proves you are controlled by sin, living like people only of
this world.
(1 Corinthians 3:3)

PSALM 74:9

We have no more miracles,
no prophets left in our midst,
nobody knows how long this will last.

This is a spiritual account of going back to square one. Perhaps this was one of the first songs sung by the Israelites in their Babylonian captivity, after their temple was destroyed. They remembered the things they knew as signs of God among them: not just the temple building, but the strong herald voice of the prophets, and the wondrous deeds of God in their daily lives. Their only certainty is uncertainty, a circumstance in which people can still find themselves today. Like the psalmist, what we must long for, more than architectural glory or any kind of power, is the restored presence of God-with-us.

PRAYER

Help me to remember, Lord,
the wisdom you have spoken,
the marvels you have worked for me.
In days of trial, let me turn to you
and never forget you.

LIVING THE PRAYER

Today I will recall a prophetic voice or a wonderful deed from God to help me through troubled times.
Am I truly grateful for the witnesses to God's grace that I have been given? Will I turn back to these when things aren't going so well?

THE NEW TESTAMENT SINGS

I want you to recall what the prophets said long ago, and what our Lord and Savior has commanded you through the apostles.
(2 Peter 3:2)

PSALM 75:1

We give you thanks, O God,
for your name is near;
all people declare your wondrous deeds.

*Two very close spiritual partners in the psalms are praise and
thankfulness. But they are not the same thing. Praise imbues the
whole psalter, even when in its language the psalm is doubting,
angry, or cheerless. Gratitude is given when God mediates a
troublesome situation to the benefit of the chosen people. Praise
is given because God is God. Thanks are given when God acts.
The opening of this psalm illustrates a deep faith in the power
of God's name to intervene; it does not describe a particular
circumstance (the vanquishing of enemies, the end of sickness).
It provides us a model of remembrance and anticipation of God's
wondrous works on our behalf.*

PRAYER

I give you thanks, O God.
How marvelous is the life you gave me,
how endless your power to work wonders.
I proclaim your name with a grateful heart.

LIVING THE PRAYER

*Today I will recall a bad time changed by God's wonderful
intervention.*
How has God blessed my life? Have there been times when
God has kept me from acting in a sinful, harmful way? Was I
grateful?

THE NEW TESTAMENT SINGS

Always give thanks for everything to God the Father, in the name
of our Lord Jesus Christ.
(Ephesians 5:20)

PSALM 76:10

Even our human wrath will give you praise,
the remnant of our wrath will gird you.

*From the beginning, human beings haven't liked to deal with
their limitations. Our bodies are limited, our days are limited,
and the energy we can expend on anything is limited. So we
need to set priorities, and we proclaim to the world, by the time
and energy we spend, what is important to us. Wrath and anger
and other negative human emotions take up quite a bit of energy,
and rob us of the energy we need to give praise to God. But the
day of the final fullness of God's reign will be marked by even
our raging fury being turned into exaltation, the last scrap of
our wrath becoming part of God's glorious raiment: our eternal
praise.*

PRAYER

Turn me away, O Lord,
from all that is hurtful or harmful.
Let me turn instead to you
and your ways, praising you alone,
and proclaiming your glory.

LIVING THE PRAYER

*Today I will redirect some negative energy or emotion into
something good for God's will.*
What unproductive or unfruitful things do I do every day that
sap my energy? How might that energy be utilized in a better
way for the work of God's reign?

THE NEW TESTAMENT SINGS

Rid yourselves of all bitterness, rage or anger, fighting and slander,
and with them every kind of malice.
(Ephesians 4:31)

PSALM 77:6

In the night I will remember my song;
>   I will meditate in my heart, my spirit ponders.

*Though studies report an increase in sleeplessness among people
in contemporary society, it was not unknown in the psalms.
The singers of Israel's songs lie awake pondering God's wonders,
or in anguish over the trials God seems to have brought, or here
taking on the futile task of trying to figure out exactly how God's
ways do get worked out in the world. We all wrestle with this
celestial insomnia from time to time, and there doesn't seem to
be a cure. Perhaps the best thing to do is to nestle ourselves deep
down into the trust, faith, and security that God's abiding love
and faithfulness provide for us.*

PRAYER

Bring me to a tranquil slumber,
God who watches over me day and night.
Hold me in your hand
and bless me with your love.

LIVING THE PRAYER

*Today, at bedtime, I will consecrate myself completely to God's
faithful, loving protection.*
What keeps me awake at night? Struggles of the day?
Worries about tomorrow? An increasing inability to shut
down? Do I trust God enough to turn over all of these to
God's care?

THE NEW TESTAMENT SINGS

"The reign of God is like the farmer who scatters his seed.
Night and day, asleep or awake, it sprouts and grows, though he
does not comprehend how."
(Mark 4:26–27)

PSALM 78:2

I will speak now in a parable.
I will teach hidden lessons from our past.

Remembrance and storytelling were two of the foundations upon which the beliefs presented in Israel's songbook were built. Since many if not most of the psalms originated and were preserved in oral tradition before they were written down, these skills were important to the faith of the tribes, and their preservation into future generations. These things were known "by heart" and were part of the heart of the people's religion. In a world and culture that always prizes the new or novel and relies on documentation, it becomes a risk that the heritage of our own faith may be preserved, but will not be pulsing through our own memories, our own stories, or our own hearts.

PRAYER

I remember your many wonders
and I tell of your saving deeds,
O Lord of faithfulness and love.
Let me announce your name
to future generations.

LIVING THE PRAYER

Today I will share a memory or a story from my faith tradition with someone else.
What are some of the scripture stories I know best?
What memories of my faith were shared with me by past generations? Do I really know them "by heart" today?

THE NEW TESTAMENT SINGS

I believe it right to keep refreshing your memory while I dwell in the tent of my earthly body.
(2 Peter 1:13)

PSALM 79:5

How long, O LORD? Will you be angry forever?
Will your jealousy continue to burn like fire?

*Of the many traits attributed to God in the Hebrew scriptures,
perhaps jealousy is the one we wrestle with the most. In human
beings, we view it as a flaw or character defect. But the jealousy
of Israel's God was one more sign of the great treasure of the
loving and faithful covenant they had together. When this love
and faithfulness were violated, God got jealous and God got
angry. We, like the scolded child or the untrustworthy spouse,
want to know when the wrath will end, sometimes forgetting
that we were the ones who caused it in the first place.*

PRAYER

May I never give you cause
for anger or jealousy, my merciful God.
Keep me faithful to you,
for I know your love lasts forever.

LIVING THE PRAYER

Today I will turn away from an act of unfaithfulness.
Do I see the love of God for me in the gifts of my daily life
and the people I love? In what ways am I unfaithful to them
or the God who has given them to me?

THE NEW TESTAMENT SINGS

Do we dare rouse the Lord's jealousy? Do we think we are stronger
than the Lord?
(1 Corinthians 10:22)

PSALM 80:8

You brought a vine out of Egypt,
drove the nations out from the land and
planted it there.

The image of us as the Lord's vine is, in a way, as unflattering as being the Lord's flock. Vines, just like sheep, need a lot of care if they are going to thrive and bear fruit (and provide wine!). Once planted, they need much careful tending. They cannot be left to their own devices, or they will run wild, a tangled mess overgrowing the place they're planted (and not bearing much fruit), even choking themselves to death. They flourish better when given a structure to grow on—better yet, a sheltered place behind a wall. Yet the fruit they bear, and the wine for the blessing cup, are worthy, treasured, and cherished in God's eyes.

PRAYER

You tend to me with a careful hand,
and nurture me to bear fruit
for the sake of your reign,
my loving, life-giving God.

LIVING THE PRAYER

Today I will allow God to prune back some part of me that has grown into a tangle.
Is there a part of my life that started out healthy, but has grown out of control and away from God? How can I still thrive but trim it back?

THE NEW TESTAMENT SINGS

A branch completely cut off from the vine will not bear fruit, and you cannot remain fruitful unless you remain in me. (John 15:4)

PSALM 81:3

Blow the shofar at the new moon,
  when the moon is full, on the great feast day!

Most of us hear horns blown on the expressway or perhaps at a sports arena. The loud and startling sound of the ram's horn was used by Israel to announce that God was doing something new, even the start of a new season indicated by the moon the Creator placed in the sky. Jews still blow the shofar on their New Year, Rosh Hashanah, and Christians hear the prophet Joel at the start of Lent tell them to be startled into a new time of grace. Even without a shofar in hand (or in our ears), we all need these "wake-up calls" from God.

PRAYER

Begin something new in me;
begin it today, O Lord.
Rouse me and startle me,
so that I may be a herald of your grace.

LIVING THE PRAYER

Today I will wake up part of my spiritual life, beginning it anew for God.
Is there an old promise or spiritual resolution I made that I no longer observe? Instead of "blowing my own horn," can it announce God's presence?

THE NEW TESTAMENT SINGS

And the Lord will come down from heaven, with a shout, with the voice of an archangel, and with the blast of a trumpet; and those who died in Christ shall rise first.
(1 Thessalonians 4:16)

PSALM 82:7

But you, O "gods," will die like mere mortals;
you will fall, like every other ruler.

*The first two commandments of Israel's covenant were
serious and forceful. It didn't matter who was in competition
with their one, true God—whether it was a god from a
neighboring religion or a mortal, earthly ruler who wanted
them to pay tribute—none other than their living, loving God
would be with them forever. Even though our own understanding
or image of God may not be as intensely jealous as Israel's,
the truth remains that anything we set up in competition
(popularity, money or other possessions, status) with the God
who is joined to us in a covenant of love will, ultimately, fail
us and abandon us. God alone will never fail.*

PRAYER

Sometimes I am quick
to find other gods for my life,
others beside you, Lord of love,
who alone will be with me always.
Bring me to your side now and forever.

LIVING THE PRAYER

*Today I will identify or recall a false god, an idol who will
abandon me or who did fail me.*
Have I placed other people or things in the place of honor
that belongs to God alone? Do I sometimes use my religion
or faith to rationalize having done so?

THE NEW TESTAMENT SINGS

Everyone tells us how you turned away from idols and turned to
serve the living and true God.
(1 Thessalonians 1:9)

PSALM 83:16

Fill the faces of your enemies with shame,
so they will seek your name, O LORD.

We sometimes begin conversations with others with an observation about how they "look" (happy, glum, tired). When the enemies of Israel (and, therefore, God's enemies) achieved some sort of victory, they no doubt looked smug, gloating disdainfully over those they had conquered. Though we aren't looking to acquire pasture or cities from our enemies as the enemies of Israel were, it is still easy enough to feel that those who are enemies of the faithful lives we try to lead are sometimes sneering or laughing at us. This is the experience of the psalmist, who would rather the enemies' faces be downcast and shame-filled, a signal perhaps that the life lived righteously is the one through which God will be victorious.

PRAYER

Though others may laugh at me
or deride me for following you,
help me seek your face, Lord.
Let my faithfulness be my victory.

LIVING THE PRAYER

Today I will give some public witness to my faith in a place where it might bring me ridicule.
Do I live out my faith only in places where it is safe to do so? When have I lacked the courage, because I was afraid that others might disdain me?

THE NEW TESTAMENT SINGS

Blessed are you when others insult you or persecute you, or falsely say evil things about you because of me.
(Matthew 5:11)

91

PSALM 84:10

Better is one day in the courts of the LORD
    than a thousand elsewhere;
I would rather be the gatekeeper at the house of my God
    than live in the tents of the wicked.

Temple gatekeepers were pretty much like the doormen at ritzy apartment buildings: working outdoors in the elements, being the first line of defense against the weirdos trying to get in, holding a position that didn't offer much in the way of remuneration. The tents of the wicked (who, the psalms note, often prosper) on the other hand, could be quite posh to live in. But Israel's devotion to the Jerusalem temple, and their faith in the God who dwelt in its holy of holies was so great that any day spent there was better than an eternity (symbolized by the number 1,000) anywhere else.

PRAYER

How I love to be in your presence,
O God of life eternal!
I desire to dwell with you
for all my days and days to come.

LIVING THE PRAYER

Today I will allow God's presence to suspend my preoccupation with the clock.
How many clocks or calendars do I have? Am I able to allow God's presence to set aside these things?

THE NEW TESTAMENT SINGS

Do not forget this, my beloved: A day is like a thousand years to the Lord, and a thousand years is like a day.
(2 Peter 3:8)

PSALM 85:11

Truth springs up from the earth,
      righteousness looks down from the heavens.

*It's nice to be swaddled in a nice cozy blanket on a cold evening,
or wrapped in a warm hug from a loved one. In this description
of the salvation that surrounds God's saints, we are told that it
is filled with peace, justice, mercy, and love. As God's chosen,
holy ones, we have been completely enveloped from the earth
below with God's truth, and from the heavens above with divine
righteousness. This also characterizes the lives of the saints who
live in God's salvation: While they walk the earth they live in
truth, and their righteous lives continue to shine on us after they
depart.*

PRAYER

You clothe your saints
with your own righteousness,
with your very truth, O Lord.
May I live and walk each day
among your holy blessed ones.

LIVING THE PRAYER

*Today I will feel myself encircled in God's love and grace through
the holy people in my life.*
Whom do I know—living or deceased—who has walked in
God's truth and righteousness? How can their witness help my
own godly living?

THE NEW TESTAMENT SINGS

Therefore, because we are surrounded by the great cloud of
witnesses, let us discard everything that burdens us and the sin
that snares us, and let us steadfastly run the race set for us.
(Hebrews 12:1)

PSALM 86:11

Teach me your way, LORD,
       so I may walk in your truth;
grant me an undivided heart,
       so I may fear your name.

Oneness, or unity, has been an oddly elusive goal for the religions that worship one God. The reasons for this are truly complex, but this psalm offers one reason that may be foundational: our failure to have truly undivided, unified hearts so that we may learn the ways of the Lord. Perhaps one of the most difficult things for us to do is to set our selfish ways aside for this purpose. It is doubtful that any unity—in our own lives, in our own faith communities, and in the larger communities or societies to which we belong— will be possible without every heart being one in offering honor and glory, and in standing in awe before the Lord.

PRAYER

Unite my whole heart
so that I may offer it to you, Lord.
Let me strive to be one
with all who honor and glorify you.

LIVING THE PRAYER

Today I will reach out to become one in faith with somebody from whom I've been estranged.
Do I ever ask others to pray with me? If not, why?

THE NEW TESTAMENT SINGS

May they know such perfect unity, so the world will know that you sent me, and that your love for them is as great as it is for me. (John 17:23)

PSALM 87:7

Those who sing and those who play the flute will say,
"The fountains of my joy are in you, Jerusalem."

Many great cities have had songs written about them. In the United States New York, Chicago, and San Francisco may come to mind. But the source of the psalmists' joy, the joy that prompted them to have a chorus and orchestra for Jerusalem, wasn't the city itself (which could have been a kind of idolatry), but the city as the central dwelling place of God, a fountain of life-giving water. We may have our own local sacred places or sites that are special for us. But first and foremost, the joy and holiness that we know in these places must come from knowing that God is present there.

PRAYER

Every joy in my life
springs from you, God whom I worship.
May I know you and love you
every place, every day.

LIVING THE PRAYER

Today I will visit one of my sacred places to give God a moment of joyful praise.
In what places do I feel closest to God in prayer, praise, or worship? Do I find a joyful fountain there for my spirit?

THE NEW TESTAMENT SINGS

I heard what sounded like a vast multitude, like the thunder of rushing waters, like great peals of thunder shouting: "Hallelujah! Our Lord God, the Almighty, reigns!"
(Revelation 19:6)

PSALM 88:18

You have taken away my companions and my loved ones;
the darkness is my only friend.

*The conclusion of this psalm, among the bleakest lines in the
psalter, has caused much consternation among commentators
and scholars. Some say the end of the manuscript has been lost,
others say that in the oral tradition (where the psalms originated)
they would have automatically added the concluding statement
of faith and praise that appears at the end of the other laments.
Probably the most difficult interpretation for this, or any Spirit-
inspired scripture, is to say, "We don't know." All that this verse
tells us is that even when we are isolated (by God's hand) and
in complete darkness, the one we still speak to is our loving,
faithful, God.*

PRAYER

Let me know my limits;
help me to leap in faith
when knowledge fails me,
loving, faithful God.

LIVING THE PRAYER

*Today I will recall or embrace a moment of total darkness; I will
turn it over to God.*
What have been the bleakest and loneliest moments of my
life? Have I been able to call out from the darkness, believing
that God still hears me?

THE NEW TESTAMENT SINGS

At the place Jesus had been crucified there was a garden, and in
that garden there was a tomb, in which no one else had ever been
laid.
(John 19:41)

PSALM 89:3

The LORD said, "I have made a covenant with David, my chosen,
I have sworn an oath to him."

In the three thousand years or so since David sat on the royal throne, the story of salvation has been filled with many surprises about what a covenant means, what it means to be chosen by God, what it means for God's sworn covenant promise to be fulfilled. It's a human tendency to think that these things mean that the chosen will get positions of authority, can do no wrong, will always be popular, will always have it easy, will never break the rules. But the story often plays out quite differently, with the only constant being God's love and faithfulness through it all. This is still God's promise today.

PRAYER

Sometimes I struggle, Lord,
to know what it means
to be your chosen one.
Help me live humbly and honestly.

LIVING THE PRAYER

Today I will live as God's chosen one in an act of humble service for others.
Do I think that being chosen by God means I always get my way, that I'm always right? Can I open up my life to live with *all* of the people whom God has chosen in this world?

THE NEW TESTAMENT SINGS

Therefore, as God's chosen ones, holy and beloved, you must clothe yourselves with compassion, kindness, humility, gentleness, and patience.
(Colossians 3:12)

PSALM 90:15

LORD, give us gladness in measure with our misery;
and good years to replace the evil ones.

*This sounds like a pretty fair bargain to strike with the
Almighty. Who, if not God, has a sense of fair play? But buried
inside this is also the awareness that permeates the psalms that
many times human beings will only learn through their misery,
and that oftentimes that misery is a result of our own tendency
to turn toward evil. But God is a God of turning back, returning,
and turning over new leaves. Also in this verse is the awareness
that our joy, too, is a vehicle for us to know and love God, the
good years of our lives providing the opportunities to offer our
praise.*

PRAYER

Though I may have done evil
and earned my misery,
help me return to you, O Lord,
my joy and my gladness.

LIVING THE PRAYER

*Today I will make a moment of gladness and goodness to give
praise to God.*
Has my misery been a result of my turning away from God?
Do I allow my return to be a time of joy and a return to
goodness as well?

THE NEW TESTAMENT SINGS

Do not imitate evil, but good. Whoever does what is good comes
from God. Whoever does what is evil has not seen God.
(3 John 1:11)

PSALM 91:6

You need not fear the pestilence stalking the darkness,
nor the disasters that strike at midday.

*Nighttime was a very fearsome time in the ancient world.
When it got dark it was* dark. *If you had a campfire or an oil
lamp, that was something, but the light they cast didn't go far
and spent very limited, precious resources. There wasn't a wall
switch nearby one could just flick on. To pass through the night
and greet the new day was something genuinely to praise God
for. Daytime was better—you could see things clearly, but your
enemies could see you more clearly, too. So it seems that we're
in need of a round-the-clock protector, one who can keep us safe
from what we can't see and from what we can!*

PRAYER

I know that you are with me
through the night
and during the day,
O Lord who watches over me,
protects me, and guides me.

LIVING THE PRAYER

*Today I will consecrate a moment of daylight and a moment of
darkness to being thankful for God's protection.*
When I awake, am I thankful that God has seen me through
another night? When my day is over, am I also grateful?

THE NEW TESTAMENT SINGS

Day after day, night after night, they say "Holy, Holy, Holy is
the Lord God Almighty, the one who was, who is, and who is to
come."
(Revelation 4:8)

PSALM 92:14

Even in old age the godly ones will produce fruit;
they will remain vital and green.

*In Israel's mostly-agrarian world, the concern for staying young
was not for external appearances, as it is in our world, but in
order to remain productive or fruitful. (One translation of this
psalm says the godly will still be "full of sap.") There is a kind
of perpetual youth to be enjoyed in living the godly life, spent
in prayer, worship, and meditation, doing good works on behalf
of others, always seeking God's way in our lives. Our faces may
still wrinkle, our bones shrink a bit, our muscles ache, but the
world around us will still benefit from the vitality of God's spirit
in us, and will be more verdant for our presence.*

PRAYER

Giver of all my days,
you are my joy.
Help me live as you desire,
and be fruitful for the kingdom.

LIVING THE PRAYER

Today I will bear some fruit for the reign of God.
What can I do, how can I live, so that others will know God's
abundant life? When I act in a godly way, do I also give God
the glory? Or do I claim credit for my good deeds?

THE NEW TESTAMENT SINGS

The fruit of the Spirit is love, joy, peace, patience, kindness,
goodness, and faithfulness.
(Galatians 5:22)

PSALM 93:4

Mightier than the violent raging of the seas,
mightier than its pounding waves,
mightier than these is the LORD on high!

One of the poetic ways the psalms like to emphasize a point is by three-fold repetition incorporating the same word or phrase or concept. This is partly because ancient languages weren't necessarily adept at things like superlatives (mighty, mightier, mightiest), but mostly because, especially in something like a psalm of praise, they weren't very interested in economy or efficiency of language. "God is mightiest" would have met with the psalmists' agreement, but the way it is expressed here would have met with agreement and approval. It seems right, perhaps, that a God who is so lavish in bestowing life and the covenant deserves some lavish language!

PRAYER

Open my heart, God of life and love.
Make my praise of you
as rich and abundant
as all the gifts you bestow.

LIVING THE PRAYER

Today I will be more extravagant in my prayer.
Do I try to "economize" when I offer my prayer and meditation to God? What about on the Lord's Day? Am I grudging with my time even then?

THE NEW TESTAMENT SINGS

I have come so that all may have life, and have it abundantly.
(John 10:10)

PSALM 94:20

Can a corrupted throne be your ally, LORD?
One that brings misery to others by its decrees?

*The problem with thrones, or seats of government, or any chairs
of any sort in which authority figures sit, is that they are all
occupied by human beings. It is impossible to name any
institution that does not have some history of people seated in
power bringing misery by their authority, and worse, pretending
that this corruption is in full alliance with God's will. When
the misery caused by such corruption is evident, this psalmist
tells us to ally ourselves prophetically with the only real power:
God's will.*

PRAYER

Grant me wisdom and grace,
God of all power,
to be loving and true in all I do,
and to discern when your will is not done.

LIVING THE PRAYER

*Today I will take note of a source of corrupt authority, and will
act to bring about God's will.*
Who in the world is using God's name in a corrupt way,
bringing misery to others? What might I be able to do to
counteract or contradict this?

THE NEW TESTAMENT SINGS

Jesus called them together, saying "You know the rulers of this
world lord it over others, and officials flaunt their authority. It is
not to be so with you."
(Mark 10:42)

PSALM 95:7

The LORD is our God.
We are his people,
the flock he tends.
If today you would listen to God's voice!

The versified Bible is about five hundred years old, though the oldest of its individual books have been around (in written form) for perhaps three thousand years. Some "verses" of the Bible (like this one) defy compartmentalization. It may be the end of one sentence, a second sentence, and the beginning of a third sentence (or a separate third sentence). From Genesis through Revelation, the God of the scriptures is a talking God. The voice of God, the voice we hear from heaven is significant. But God, including God's voice in the Spirit-inspired scriptures, doesn't always speak in clearly defined units. So our task is to listen carefully and with an open heart.

PRAYER

I know that you are still speaking
in the world today, Lord.
Let me open my ears, my heart,
all my senses to your
grace-filled word.

LIVING THE PRAYER

Today I will use all my senses to "hear" God's voice.
Can I "hear" God's voice in the scent of daily bread? In the touch of an embrace or even a handshake? In the news accounts that I read or watch? How can I remain more open to God's "voice" in the world?

THE NEW TESTAMENT SINGS

Jesus called the crowd to himself, to come and hear. "Listen, all of you," he said, "so you might understand." (Mark 7:14)

PSALM 96:1

Sing a new song to the Lord;
sing to the Lord, all you on earth.

The psalms contain about half a dozen entries that admonish us to sing this "new" song, and we might think this is why there are so many psalms. We think of "new" as meaning "different" but for the scriptural authors it has more of the sense of "renewed." They lived, after all, in a world where one did not just go to the store or online to get something "new." In daily life items were used, repaired, and then re-used in their renewed form. Even if we had or only knew one song to the Lord, we could still make it "new" each day, by renewing our awareness of God's presence in our lives.

PRAYER

Renew my heart today
for your praise O my God.
Let this new day be filled
with the new song you
place on my lips.

LIVING THE PRAYER

Today I will repeat one line from a favorite hymn, finding new meaning in it each time.
Do I take a "top forty" approach to the songs I sing to the Lord? What can I do to renew the prayer of the songs I am already familiar with?

THE NEW TESTAMENT SINGS

Sing psalms and hymns and spiritual songs to God with thankful hearts.
(Colossians 3:16)

PSALM 97:10

You who love the LORD, hate evil!
    The LORD preserves the lives of godly people,
    rescuing them from the wicked.

There is a difference between hating what is evil and merely being indifferent toward it. It's even easy to be apathetic about it, we figure, as long as we are not creating the evil (or being affected by it). But just as our love of the Lord calls on us to live it out in the actions of our daily lives—being godly people—then, conversely, a real hatred of evil will lead us to acknowledge it, confront it, and work to change it as heralds of God's desire for what is true and right in the world.

PRAYER

I love you, Lord!
Help me to show my love for you
in daily deeds for justice, truth, and peace.

LIVING THE PRAYER

Today I will work to change one evil in the world.
Even if I am not successful (or can't do it alone), do I continue to work against evil? Can I recall times my inertia actually helped continue something wrong?

THE NEW TESTAMENT SINGS

The grace of God teaches us to deny ungodliness and worldly passion, to live sensible, righteous, and godly lives in our present time.
(Titus 2:11–12)

PSALM 98:7

Let the sea resound, and all that lives in it,
the world and all who live in it.

Israel did not have a modern understanding of the sheer scope of water covering the whole globe, nor of the myriad human beings scattered over the fact of the earth, but they still understood the vast waters as a place teeming with rich and mysterious life. Their own history gave them a daily experience of the diversity of peoples and cultures. Even today, "the sea" doesn't mean some pretty waves crashing on the shore; it means the whole sea praising God's salvation. "All who live in the world" doesn't mean just a few people a bit different than me; it means all the people praising God's saving power.

PRAYER

Let the horizons of my
prayer and praise grow wider,
as wide as your boundless
love, mercy, and salvation,
O Lord my God.

LIVING THE PRAYER

Today I will use a research book, Web site, or TV special to explore the vastness of life and people on earth.
How constrained are my preconceptions about God's love?
Can broadening my knowledge about the world around me broaden my understanding?

THE NEW TESTAMENT SINGS

Then I heard every creature in heaven and earth and under the earth and in the sea. They sang: "Blessing, honor, glory, and power to the one seated on the throne and to the Lamb forever and ever!" (Revelation 5:13)

PSALM 99:7

The LORD spoke from the pillar of cloud,
and Israel followed the laws and
decrees given to them.

*The pillars of cloud and fire that traveled through the desert
with the people of Israel remained emblems of their faithful
God, the one who stayed with them throughout that great time
of trial and preparation for entering the Promised Land. Many
of us, if we had something as remarkable as a talking cloud,
would certainly follow any laws or decrees we received from it!
But—absence of cloudy/fiery pillars notwithstanding—we all
have signs (some of them pretty marvelous, if we stop to think
about it) in our lives of faith that are markers of God whom we
trust to remain with us, to guide us through life's journey.*

PRAYER

Be with me, remain with me
in the signs of love you have given me.
Let me follow your way,
wherever my life might lead.

LIVING THE PRAYER

*Today I will recall signs of God's presence with me, and will pay
heed to them.*
When or where have I seen or known the presence of God?
Did I stay with it faithfully? If not, can I do so at this point in
my life?

THE NEW TESTAMENT SINGS

A cloud overshadowed them, and a voice from the cloud said,
"This is my beloved Son. Listen to him."
(Mark 9:7)

PSALM 100:4

Enter God's gates with thanksgiving;
enter God's courts with praise.
Give thanks, and bless his holy name.

This is an etiquette primer on how one goes about calling upon the divine majesty. Unlike going to the court of an earthly ruler, we enter the gates (the outer boundary of the palace) not with written proof of identification or citizenship; our thanksgiving identifies us. We do not enter into the royal throne room bearing precious gifts or offerings; we bear only our unconditional praise. Nor do we come into the divine presence speaking our desires or wants or requests for favors, for God knows these already. All we must do is bless God's holy name, the name that has the wisdom and the will to receive us and grant us what we truly need.

PRAYER

I come into your presence,
Lord God my King,
offering my thanks and praise,
blessing your name
as I pray to you.

LIVING THE PRAYER

Today I will put aside all extraneous things that I think I need to do in God's presence.
What hoops do I think I must jump through to come before God? How can I rid myself of them?

THE NEW TESTAMENT SINGS

Are any among you suffering? Then let them pray. Are any cheerful? They are to sing praises.
(James 5:13)

PSALM 101:2

I will attentively lead a blameless life—
        when, O L<small>ORD</small>, will you come to me?
I will walk in my house
        with a heart full of integrity.

It doesn't seem like much of an accomplishment to maintain integrity while walking around your own house. But a biblical "house" is not just the domicile where we reside. It represents the fullness of our lives, everything and every responsibility given to us. The second half of this verse is echoing the first half. By leading the blameless life we are doing our housecleaning so that we may receive the Lord. It is this house filled with blamelessness and integrity that truly welcomes the Lord, and leads the Lord—one day—to welcome us to dwell in a heavenly home for eternity.

PRAYER

Let me serve only you, my Lord.
Keep me blameless and upright,
so that I may come to live
in your house forever.

LIVING THE PRAYER

Today I will tend to one overdue "housecleaning" task.
Is my spiritual house in order and ready to receive the Lord?
If not, what cleanup needs to be done?

THE NEW TESTAMENT SINGS

You, then, as living stones, are being built up as a spiritual house for this holy priesthood, where you offer spiritual sacrifice acceptable to God through Christ Jesus.
(1 Peter 2:5)

PSALM 102:13

You will arise, LORD, and have compassion on Zion,
for it is time to show her your favor;
the appointed hour is now here.

*For anyone living with an "all things in God's own time"
mindset, this verse seems like a rather pushy way to address
God. But this psalm is written from a very troubled place.
Perhaps in thinking of someone diagnosed with a terminal
illness, facing an unexpected divorce, or some other time of
trial, this becomes more understandable. It seems to be at these
moments that we need to remind ourselves (and if God hears it,
too, so much the better) that every moment of our life is a good
time for God's compassionate love to shine. Indeed, every time is
filled with this possibility, for the Lord is ever-compassionate.*

PRAYER

Let your grace, favor, and compassion
be showered on me, O Lord.
In times of trouble, in times of joy,
you are always my loving savior.

LIVING THE PRAYER

*Today I will take a time—happy or sad—to be open to God's care
for me.*
How can I remain open at every moment to receive God's
mercy? Can I do this even when my life is not in turmoil?

THE NEW TESTAMENT SINGS

Praised be the God and Father of our Lord Jesus Christ, Father of
all compassion, God of all comfort.
(2 Corinthians 1:3)

PSALM 103:4

The LORD redeems your life from destruction,
and crowns you with loving-kindness and
compassion.

*Most of us might prefer that God crown us with a real crown,
not being sufficiently grateful that God has redeemed us from
destruction (or "the pit" or death, in other translations). But
this points up once again why God redeems us and saves us in
the first place. It is not so that God can look good, or so that
we can somehow lord it over others, but so that we can live in
the world with God's traits: the loving-kindness of the covenant
and the compassion for the poor, hungry, marginalized, and
oppressed who might need to find God's redemption through our
action on their behalf.*

PRAYER

Crown me with your crown, O Lord,
the crown of mercy, love, justice, and peace.
Let me show your redemption
in the life I live for others.

LIVING THE PRAYER

Today I will show my "crown" of God's love and compassion.
Does my belief in God's redemption show itself in my
attitude of humble service? Or am I smug, self-righteous,
or self-serving?

THE NEW TESTAMENT SINGS

There is a crown of righteousness awaiting me, which the Lord,
the righteous Judge, will bestow on me one day—not only to me,
but to all those who have longed for his coming.
(2 Timothy 4:8)

PSALM 104:2

The LORD is wrapped in light as with a cloak,
and stretches out the heavens like a tent.

*It is a bit quirky that this psalm, one of the most glorious
retellings of the wonders of creation, starts off with this "just
one of us" depictions of the Creator. Israelites knew what it was
to be dressed in a cloak, and to dwell in a tent. Granted, the
Lord is dressed in light itself and dwells in the heavens, but
the humanizing image is heartening as well. We are made in
the image of this "one of us" God, and it is not beyond our
abilities—or God's expectations for us—to share in the wonder
of the divine life- and light-giving creation.*

PRAYER

How wonderful you are, O Lord!
You spoke and there was light
and there was life;
let me still bring them into the world
as a sign of your love.

LIVING THE PRAYER

Today I will let the glory of God's creation shine for others.
How can I reveal the love of God by sharing some wonder of
creation? Does my life as a wise steward show this same love?

THE NEW TESTAMENT SINGS

For God's unseen qualities—eternal power and divine nature—
have clearly been seen since the creation of the world, in all things
that have been made.
(Romans 1:20)

PSALM 105:45

So Israel would keep the LORD's precepts,
and follow his commands.
Praise the LORD!

*This psalm is a history lesson, recounting the covenant with
Israel's patriarchs and the time of Egyptian slavery and Exodus.
At the very conclusion, we find out why God did all this,
why all this happened. Not because God is so great or loving,
or as a reward for Israel's perseverance. All of this happened
so Israel would keep the laws of the Lord, and follow faithfully
in their ways. Though God does act out of love and desires our
faithfulness, the ultimate "prize" for us is to follow God's will
steadfastly—and joyfully! This is why this psalm ends with
Israel's classic expression of praise: Hallelu Yah!*

PRAYER

Hallelujah!
I praise you, Lord,
for every good thing.
Help me follow your commands
with a faithful, joyful heart.

LIVING THE PRAYER

*Today I will allow God's goodness to deepen my desire to follow
God's commands.*
When I think of the good God has done for me, do I think
it's because of my own goodness? Do I allow my thankfulness
to spur me on to action?

THE NEW TESTAMENT SINGS

And this is love itself: to walk in obedience to God's commands.
(2 John 1:6)

PSALM 106:13

But soon they had forgotten what God had done
for them;
and they did not listen to God's counsel.

Israel, like the rest of us, turned to God most often when they
were in trouble, in danger, in exile, or grieving. They were fully
confident that God's loving-kindness and merciful love would
always be there for them. "How quickly they forget" applies
here as well. How often we still find ourselves in trouble or need
because we have forgotten what God has had to do for us in the
past; because we forget to heed the wisdom that God has given
us time and time again! How often our relationship with God
gets re-energized because of our short attention span.

PRAYER

Help me remember
your wondrous deeds
and your mighty wisdom, O Lord.
Keep them before me
every day of my life.

LIVING THE PRAYER

Today I will stop myself from doing something I know—
from past experience—is not God's will.
In the past, what actions or thoughts have led me to stumble
in God's ways? Do I still repeat them? How can I be more open
to God's wisdom and God's voice?

THE NEW TESTAMENT SINGS

Jesus said: "Have you forgotten my breaking the five loaves for
five thousand, and how many baskets of bread you picked up?"
They replied, "Twelve."
(Mark 8:18–19)

PSALM 107:17

Some turned into fools through their defiant ways;
  they suffered misery due to their transgressions.

*We can get pretty smug in our own time and place, thinking
we now understand that suffering is not necessarily a divine
punishment or retribution for sinfulness. But this should not
lead us to think that our transgressions do not or will not have
consequences. It is still true that defying the will of God in the
way we live is, ultimately, a stupid thing to do. And our patterns
of unhealthy or sinful behaviors and actions are still a sure way
down the road of misery. But God always stands at the ready
to save us from our sins, which often means saving us from
ourselves.*

PRAYER

Keep me from my foolish ways,
save me from the suffering
that I often bring upon myself;
for you, O Lord, are the source
of all grace and life.

LIVING THE PRAYER

*Today I will identify and start working to end one thing that defies
God.*
When I examine my daily life, what patterns emerge that lead
me away from God? How can I allow God's grace to re-direct
me?

THE NEW TESTAMENT SINGS

The merciful God made us alive with Christ though we were dead
in transgressions; by grace we have been saved.
(Ephesians 2:5)

PSALM 108:2
Awake, harp and lyre!
I will awaken the dawn!

The psalmists liked to speak in extremes. In their world, very nearly everyone and everything got up at the crack of dawn. Even in urban areas, there were enough animals and their keepers to put the whole city on a rural time clock. The dawn did the awakening, not the other way around. But here the psalmist is so excited, so overflowing with the song of God's praise that the everyday starting time can't be observed. It is so urgent and important that even one's inanimate musical instruments are roused to praise their Maker. Singing God's praise is everyone's glorious alarm clock!

PRAYER

As you waken me each day,
let my first thought and act
be your praise, O Lord.
Let your light dawn in my life!

LIVING THE PRAYER

Today I will resolve to begin the day in prayer
In the list of activities that begin my day, when is my first prayer to God? Even if brief, can I make this my first activity each day?

THE NEW TESTAMENT SINGS

It is the light that makes all things visible. For this reason we say: "Awake, O sleeper, arise from the dead; and Christ will shine on you."
(Ephesians 5:14)

PSALM 109:28

Others may curse me, but you bless me;
>   when they assault me, they will be put to shame,
>   I rejoice, for I am your servant.

It's difficult to know whether or not we're acting in a prophetic manner. The prophets often came under attack and were ostracized, but that doesn't mean that every time that others assail us we've been acting prophetically. Sometimes people treat us that way because we're being jerks. Figuring out the difference calls upon us to have a spirit of discernment. The psalmist assures us, however, that when we have been acting righteously and according God's will, we are blessed, even though others revile and curse us. Ultimately, God will be in charge; our truest joy is being the Lord's servants.

PRAYER

Lead me to do your will, O God.
Help me to act righteously,
so that when others berate me
I can rejoice, living faithfully.

LIVING THE PRAYER

Today I will try to determine whether I am living in a truly prophetic manner.
Do others criticize me or ridicule me for things I do? Are these things that I do to live out the will of God, or do I do them for the wrong reasons?

THE NEW TESTAMENT SINGS

As an example, then, of suffering and patience, we have the prophets, who spoke in the name of the Lord.
(James 5:10)

PSALM 110:7

The Lord will drink from the brook by the wayside;
therefore will his head be lifted up.

*This is a "double Lord" psalm: it refers to the LORD (God) and
the Lord (the anointed king, the psalmist's boss). It can be a bit
confusing to figure out which Lord is being spoken of. At the end
of the psalm, it is the second one. Since this psalm is a military
war song, this concluding verse describes two things that an
ancient warrior didn't do: stop by a frequented place (a brook
along the wayside) and expose vulnerability (lifting up his
head). Yet, in a brave, bold demonstration of faith and trust in
the LORD God, this is exactly what this human "lord" does.*

PRAYER

My faith and trust in you
is complete, O Lord my God.
It is you who refresh my soul,
and you who raise me up
to new life.

LIVING THE PRAYER

*Today I will allow myself to trust in God when I'm in a precarious
situation.*
Do I believe that God watches over me? What sort of things
that happen in my daily life might be easier if I truly trusted in
God?

THE NEW TESTAMENT SINGS

When you see the Son of Man coming, arise and lift up your heads,
for your redemption is at hand.
(Luke 21:28)

PSALM 111:10

Fear of the LORD is the beginning of wisdom;
those who practice it come
to a good understanding.
The praise of the LORD endures forever!

*"Fear" in scriptural language is a problematic term for some
people. This may be because most commonly in current usage it
means only "afraid." Some modern Bible translations use "awe"
or "respect" or similar terms; but those are inadequate as well.
It is a mixture of wonder and humble obedience and a sense of
our own peril when we ignore the Lord that begins our wisdom.
And we must remember that this is only the first step in our
"practice" of it!*

PRAYER

Lead me in your wisdom, O Lord.
Let me know your might,
show me your splendor,
guide me in humility,
bring me to live in your love.

LIVING THE PRAYER

*Today I will think of God's might, splendor, and holiness as my
way to grow in wisdom.*
Do I comprehend the risk of not living in an ongoing, growing
understanding of God? Can I integrate the various aspects of
what the Bible calls "fear" of the Lord?

THE NEW TESTAMENT SINGS

If you are willing to do the will of God, then you will know
whether my wisdom is truly from God, or if I am merely speaking
on my own authority.
(John 7:17)

PSALM 112:9

The righteous give generously to the poor,
    their righteousness will last forever;
    their dignity will be held high in honor.

*Some translations of this verse speak of the righteous scattering
their gifts abroad—a seed-sowing image. Perhaps the lasting
nature of the legacy of our generous giving can be thought of
as the forest or field of flowers that, once sown, flourishes
perpetually. The psalmist does not promise that generosity
to the poor guarantees fame or an in-kind return on the
investment, but that when we act in righteous charity,
we can initiate a process that—though we may not witness
it firsthand—bears much fruit.*

PRAYER

Let me see you
in the poor of the world,
my loving Lord.
Help me always to act righteously
and generously toward them.

LIVING THE PRAYER

Today I will perform an act of charitable generosity for the poor.
Do I give to others only from my excess? Even if my means
are limited, what amount or action can I offer to alleviate the
suffering of poverty?

THE NEW TESTAMENT SINGS

Some of the apostles asked only that we remember the poor—
the very thing I was eager to do.
(Galatians 2:10)

PSALM 113:7

[The LORD] raises the poor from the dust,
and lifts the needy from the ash heap.

An ash heap back then was pretty much what it is now—
a burned-out place. Ash heaps were places where campfires had
been built and meals enjoyed. The poorest of the poor searched
them in hopes of finding a small, still-warm ember, or a scrap
that had not been consumed. They did this before they slept
on the barren, dusty earth. For the deities of the surrounding
nations, these people were beneath notice, and societies tended
(and still do) to treat them the same way. Yet it is among these
very people that God's saving power is witnessed.

PRAYER

God of the poor and lowly,
help me see the world
with your eyes
and your saving power
not with the mighty, but with the helpless.

LIVING THE PRAYER

Today I will be a witness to God's favor for the weak, poor, or
lowly.
What have I done, or what can I do, to be an agent for a God
who raises up the lowly and speaks out for the oppressed? In
what ways have I failed to act when given the opportunity?

THE NEW TESTAMENT SINGS

Truly, I say that what you did for the least of these, my sisters and
brothers, you did for me.
(Matthew 25:40)

PSALM 114:4

The mountains skipped like rams,
the hills leapt like young lambs.

When the psalmist wanted to describe the joy that the very earth experienced when the Lord's flock was released from its Egyptian slavery, it was with this most extremely playful contrast. Two of the mightiest and most stable geographical features of the land were jumping about like the two most feisty and frolicsome members of the flock. It is the rams and the lambs that tend to be the most spontaneously active (and unpredictably unmanageable). Nor did the mountains—and their smaller offspring, the hills—do a well-choreographed courtly dance; they bounded about capriciously.

PRAYER

Fill me with joy, my God!
Let your saving love
cause me to leap and shout
and sing your praise,
so that all may come to know and love you.

LIVING THE PRAYER

Today I will express my joy in God's love in an outward, noticeable way.
Do I think it sufficient to keep my joy at God's presence inside? Am I more afraid that others will find my behavior suspect than I am confident of God's salvation?

THE NEW TESTAMENT SINGS

Every time I pray for all of you, my prayer is filled with joy.
(Philippians 1:4)

PSALM 115:2
Why do all the peoples exclaim, "Where is their God?"

When the psalmist wrote this question, it was in the context of other religions that made many images or idols of their gods, something that Israel prohibited. So naturally, others would wonder where Israel's God might be, the God who could only be "seen" in the lives and witness of the Chosen People. People can still rightly ask this question of us today, when they fail to see God alive and active in us. They can also ask the question when it seems that affluence or success or possessions or popularity or any number of things are false gods in our lives.

PRAYER
Fill my every
thought, word, and deed
with your loving presence, Lord.
Let others see your glory
shining through me.

LIVING THE PRAYER
Today I will let God's presence be seen in my actions.
What small way will there be today for me to let God's love
and grace shine forth? Are there things in my life that others
could mistake for my real gods?

THE NEW TESTAMENT SINGS
Let your light shine before the world, so others may see your good
deeds and give glory to your Father in heaven.
(Matthew 5:16)

PSALM 116:8

For you [, Lord,] have delivered my soul from death,
    my eyes from tears,
    my feet from stumbling.

*This seems like an unusual verse for a people who did not have
a well-developed concept of an immaterial spiritual entity
(a soul) going somewhere to live for eternity. But Israel
acknowledged that, made in God's image, we are more than
mere physical bodies, and when God saves us from death, it is
our whole being, our whole life, that is saved. This doesn't lead
us merely to look to a next life, but to live this one in God's joy
and steadfast love.*

PRAYER

Be with me today,
God, my life and joy.
Do not let death trap me,
but let me live in your ways.

LIVING THE PRAYER

Today I will honor God, my deliverer.
When have I been spared something unfortunate?
Did I breathe a sigh of relief, or use my breath to glorify God,
who delivered me? When telling others, did I acknowledge
God's hand?

THE NEW TESTAMENT SINGS

And God will wipe away every tear; and there will no longer be
any death; nor mourning nor crying, nor pain; for the first things
have passed away.
(Revelation 21:4)

PSALM 117:1

Praise the LORD, all you nations;
glorify the LORD, all you peoples.

Most of the deities in the ancient world were portrayed as capable of being capricious, playing with peoples' lives as with a game. Not so with Israel's God, who entered into a full and binding covenant with the Chosen People. When the nation of Israel exhorted others to praise their God, it wasn't a statement that other gods didn't exist, but rather that Israel's God was the one to praise, glorify, and follow. In this, the shortest of the psalms, the next (and final) verse explains that Israel's God, unlike the others, is loving and faithful.

PRAYER

I praise you, Lord,
source of all loving kindness
and everlasting faithfulness.
May my life lead others to
glorify you.

LIVING THE PRAYER

Today I will try to help someone else glorify God.
Do I avoid discussing the love and faithfulness of God in my life? When I give God the credit for the goodness in my life, do I do so in a way that leads others to offer praise?

THE NEW TESTAMENT SINGS

Go, then, and make disciples of every nation; baptize them in the name of the Father and the Son and the Holy Spirit. (Matthew 28:19)

PSALM 118:24

This is the day that the LORD has made;
let us rejoice and be glad in it.

*When we think of God's creation, we think mostly of those
things (animals, plants, people) named in the Genesis accounts.
How often do we recall that one of the things created by the Lord
is the day, separated from perpetual darkness of night? And even
more, do we recall that this day is God's creation only when
things are going our way? When we are happy and successful
and trouble-free? How much greater is the challenge of rejoicing
in this creation of God when life—as this whole psalm
represents it—is not so joy-filled!*

PRAYER

I thank you, I bless you,
I praise you for this day, my Lord!
Let me rejoice in its every moment,
no matter what it brings.

LIVING THE PRAYER

Today I will take several different moments to rejoice in this day.
Can I rejoice in this day after bad news or an argument? Is
it possible to offer God my joy in the middle of a boring or
tiresome task? How can I allow this joy to make ordinary days
extraordinary?

THE NEW TESTAMENT SINGS

Rejoice in that day, leap for joy; your reward in heaven is great. For
this is how their ancestors rejected the prophets.
(Luke 6:23)

PSALM 119:1

Blessed are the ones who live blamelessly,
who walk in the ways of God's law.

It's a rather daunting task, trying to find one verse to open up the longest psalm (176 verses!) in the Bible. This psalm is intended to be a summary of all of Israel's wisdom about faithfully following God's ways. It is no coincidence that its beginning resonates with Psalm 1, the opening of the entire psalter. Many things in life seem daunting or overwhelming, but our tending to them begins with that proverbial first step. Our blessedness and our happiness rely on us taking that small first step in God's ways.

PRAYER

Walk with me, today, my God.
Help me face my challenges,
confident that your commands
will guide me and bless me.

LIVING THE PRAYER

Today I will take one small step with God.
What journey or task—especially a spiritual or personal one—seems too much for me? Is there one small thing that I can do that, with God's help, will set me on the right course?

THE NEW TESTAMENT SINGS

The sinful mind does not receive God; it does not submit itself to God's law, it cannot even attempt to do so.
(Romans 8:7)

PSALM 120:3

What will the LORD give to you,
or what shall be done to you,
O deceitful tongue?

Deceit is a particularly reprehensible form of falsehood in the psalms. It is no mere lie, but calculated and thoughtfully planned-out scheming. While technically this verse is praying about the deceitful tongues of others (they are punished in the next verse), it is good to remember that there is little in the scripture that we can—or ought to—pray about others that does not simultaneously include ourselves. Others may be offering this very same prayer about us!

PRAYER

Keep me mindful of my tongue today;
may I remember the harm that it can do,
the falsehood that it can promote.
Let me consecrate my every word
to your honor and glory, O Lord.

LIVING THE PRAYER

Today I will end a deceit of mine, or refuse to participate in somebody else's.
How do I deceive others at home, in school, at work, in friendships? Do I silently cooperate in others' deceits by not standing up for integrity and honesty?

THE NEW TESTAMENT SINGS

The tongue is a small part of the body, but it boasts of great things; and see how a great forest can be set aflame by a small fire! (James 3:5)

PSALM 121:8

The LORD is guardian of your going out and
your coming in,
from this time forth, forever.

*We still speak today of people's "comings and goings." That is
what is being referred to here as well: God is the guardian of
our every action. This is truly a psalm of God, the God of all:
the maker of heaven and earth, the one who protects us from
the sun and the moon, the whole day and night through. It is
easy enough to think that God only watches over us when we
are in trouble or acting sinfully, or when we pray at home or in
church, but we are reminded that God is truly with us every
moment of our lives.*

PRAYER

When I wake from sleep
until I fall asleep again,
I know you are with me, Lord.
Watch over me and guard me
all my days.

LIVING THE PRAYER

Today I will focus on God-with-me at an unusual time.
What are some daily activities that I don't think God is
necessarily interested in or tending to? How is God truly
present to me at these times?

THE NEW TESTAMENT SINGS

May the peace of God, surpassing all understanding, guard your
hearts and minds in Christ Jesus.
(Philippians 4:7)

129

PSALM 122:8

For the sake of my family and friends,
I say "Peace be within your walls."

It may seem self-serving to pray for peace only for the sake of one's family and friends, but even in our modern world, doing this is somewhat like tossing a stone into the middle of a pond. Our family members and friends have their own family members and friends to pray for. In a similar fashion, the psalm is not just praying for peace within the domestic walls, but within the walls of the city of Jerusalem, a symbol of the walls surrounding all God's chosen people. When we initiate the action of God's peace, the circle always widens.

PRAYER

Lord, let your peace come to the world
through my prayer,
in my speaking,
by my daily living.

LIVING THE PRAYER

Today I will pray for and act on behalf of peace in the world. How can praying and living for peace help my family and friends? How can it also have some effect on increasing the message of peace in a troubled world?

THE NEW TESTAMENT SINGS

This is the Good News for the people of Israel: there is peace with God through Jesus Christ, the Lord of all.
(Acts 10:36)

PSALM 123:2

As the eyes of slaves
> look to the hand of their master,
as the eyes of a maid
> look to the hand of her mistress,
so our eyes look to the LORD our God,
> till he shows us mercy.

*Though few of us have ever actually experienced a life lived in
complete servitude, much less slavery, it is still easy enough to
be enslaved by or be servile before other things besides God.
Our eyes can look relentlessly at the TV screen or the text
message screen on the cell phone. But we will never find mercy
there; those things only ask for more and more and more
servitude from us. It is better, then, to keep our eyes on the
hand of the Lord, who cares for us and shows us mercy.*

PRAYER

I am your servant,
I look to you, Lord.
Show me your mercy
and let me love you
faithfully and steadfastly.

LIVING THE PRAYER

Today I will turn away from one un-godly activity or behavior.
Where do my eyes spend most of their day? Is it someplace
where I will know the goodness or grace of God in my life?
What unhealthy "looking" do I participate in?

THE NEW TESTAMENT SINGS

"I am the handmaid of the Lord," Mary said to Gabriel. "Let it be
done to me as you have said."
(Luke 1:38)

PSALM 124:8

Our help is in the Lord's name;
the Lord who made heaven and earth.

Say out loud the name of somebody you love or admire or respect. That name calls forth a whole series of feelings, memories, and all sorts of other connections. If it is someone to whom you are particularly close, perhaps you can even feel that person's presence. This is the sort of close familial relationship that Israel had in naming God, and in calling upon God's name for help. Calling out that name brought forth the presence and memory of the mighty works God did and continues to do in the lives of faithful believers.

PRAYER

I call upon your name,
Lord my God.
You are my help,
my joy, my peace,
my love, my life.

LIVING THE PRAYER

Today I will call on the name of the Lord, out loud, in love.
Do I pray out loud when I pray alone? Why or why not? How is my personal prayer different when I give it a voice? Am I worried or perhaps embarrassed that others will hear me pray?

THE NEW TESTAMENT SINGS

Therefore let us draw confidently near to the throne of grace,
so we will receive mercy and find grace to help in our time of need.
(Hebrews 4:16)

PSALM 125:3

The scepter of wickedness shall not rest
upon the land given to the righteous,
so the righteous will not stretch out
their hand to do wrong.

No matter what form of government people live under, no matter their economic or social status, it is impossible not to get tangled up, to some degree, in the systems that run the day-to-day lives of a society. This is one of the reasons that disciples are called upon to raise a prophetic challenge whenever some rule of evil seems to be resting on the land, causing those who live there to participate in it in some way. Even if we don't hold a political office, or if we aren't in a role with great social impact, each of us can do something to counter a reign of wickedness.

PRAYER

Open my eyes, Lord,
to seek your will
for the world around me;
strengthen me.

LIVING THE PRAYER

Today I will stand up to a wrong that I encounter.
What power—small or great—do I possess that can change the world? How can I act positively in spite of feeling overwhelmed by the scale of the world's problems?

THE NEW TESTAMENT SINGS

You have loved righteousness, hated wickedness; therefore your God has set you above others, anointing you with the oil of gladness.
(Hebrews 1:9)

133

PSALM 126:2

Our mouths were filled with laughter;
on our lips were joyful songs.
Then the nations said,
"The Lord has done great things for them!"

There is a story about the philosopher Friederich Nietzsche seeing Christians coming out from church one Sunday morning and observing to a friend, "Odd. They don't look redeemed." While it is certainly not the hallmark of a Christian to wear a (suspiciously) relentless grin at all times, neither is it a badge of holiness to be dour all the time as a sign of the continual struggle between sin and grace going on inside. In addition to our witness to the work of justice and peace in the world, a cheerful face and attitude are also signs of the good news that we know to be God's truth!

PRAYER

You are the joy of my salvation,
Lord my God.
Let me delight in this day
and every day you give me
to share the Good News.

LIVING THE PRAYER

Today I will express my faith in a joyful way.
When I help others, can I do so with a smile or a cheerful word as well? Do I offer prayers of joy and gratitude in addition to all the requests for my needs? Can others detect that I've been redeemed?

THE NEW TESTAMENT SINGS

Be joyful in hope, patient in affliction, and faithful in prayer. (Romans 12:12)

PSALM 127:2

It is vain to rise early,
    to stay up late,
toiling for your food to eat—
    for God provides for those he loves, even as they sleep.

At last! A divinely-inspired mandate for sleeping in. Perfect to give to parents or bosses. This, of course, is not the intent of the psalm. And, even though the need to toil in order to stay alive was one of the punishments for the grace lost in Eden, God's providential, loving hand is also in our labors. In a world that often seems to judge us—or in which we judge ourselves— according to how "busy" or "connected" we are, it can be even more important to remember to consecrate each day, from rising to sleeping, to the God who made us, who remains with us in love.

PRAYER

Loving Creator God,
let every moment today
be pleasing to you.
May I trust in your care
and glorify you in all things.

LIVING THE PRAYER

Today I will take a moment to bless God when I rise, work, and sleep.
Do I find myself spending more time accomplishing less?
Do I try to squeeze important moments at home or at prayer between multiple tasks? What can I simply turn over to God?

THE NEW TESTAMENT SINGS

Look at how the lilies grow; they do not labor or spin. Yet not even Solomon in all his splendor was clothed like them.
(Luke 12:27)

PSALM 128:6
May you live to see your children's children,
and may peace be upon Israel.

In our day, when it's not unusual for people to live to see their children's children's children (great-grandchildren), the first part of this verse doesn't seem like the outrageous and extremely hopeful wish that it truly was when life expectancy was low and infant mortality was high. But we do have a bit more understanding of what a great blessing it would be for true peace to be upon the people and the land of Israel. For the psalmist, both of these hopes are an expression of the most profound belief and trust in the loving, blessing, and providential hand of God.

PRAYER
Gracious and generous God,
bestow peace on our troubled world,
grant abundant life to all your children,
fill the whole earth with your blessings.

LIVING THE PRAYER
Today I will look for and share God's abundant blessings.
What do I hope to live long enough to see? For myself? For the world? What can I do to help bring this about? How can I be a sign of God's plentiful grace?

THE NEW TESTAMENT SINGS
From the fullness of the grace of Christ, we have received one blessing upon another.
(John 1:16)

PSALM 129:3

The plowmen have worked my back;
they have made long furrows there.

*"Get off my back!" is an expression we still use today, though
in an increasingly urban culture, we don't think in the farming
terms used in this psalm. It is something of a curiosity that
this image wasn't among those used by Christians to understand
the suffering of Jesus. Perhaps this is due to the largely vindictive
tone of the whole psalm. Using the spiritual heritage of the
psalms in the new covenant of Christ can be something of a
challenge. We can still acknowledge the adversity that is present
in our lives without seeking the retribution that the rest of the
text seems to call for.*

PRAYER

Be my strength, O Lord.
Stay with me in times of trouble,
in my suffering or pain,
helping me to bear all things patiently.

LIVING THE PRAYER

Today I will bear some insult, injury, or suffering in patience.
When I am wronged, is my first inclination to retaliate? In
my dealings with others, am I ever the "plowman" the psalm
mentions?

THE NEW TESTAMENT SINGS

As the sufferings of Christ are ours in abundance, through Christ
our comfort is also abundant.
(2 Corinthians 1:5)

PSALM 130:5

I wait for you, Lord, my soul is waiting;
in your word I place all my hope.

*Even in our culture of multitasking, we think of "waiting" as
passive time. "I'll do _____ while I'm waiting." In scripture,
waiting for the Lord is far from a passive thing. It calls upon
us to be alive, every nerve alert for the will of God becoming
present, becoming known to us. We might even think of it more
precisely as waiting on the Lord to require something of us
(in the manner of attentive servants) than waiting for the Lord
(as we would at an airport). The psalmist's hopefulness is not
merely that eventually God will show up, but that God's word is
always alive and active.*

PRAYER

I wait for you, Lord,
with eyes, ears, mind, and heart open.
I hope in you, Lord,
ready to be your servant each day.

LIVING THE PRAYER

*Today I will wait for the Lord by listening for God's word in my
daily life.*
Do I live a hopeful life? How does my belief that God is still
speaking make me a hope-filled person? Is my "waiting" for
God's presence active or passive?

THE NEW TESTAMENT SINGS

Be like those who wait for their master to return from the wedding
feast: ready to open the door immediately when he arrives and
knocks on the door.
(Luke 12:36)

PSALM 131:2

My soul is still and quiet within me;
>like a weaned child with its mother,
>my soul within me is like a weaned child.

Few things are as restless, relentless, noisy, or selfish as a hungry infant. And that infant wants only one thing: to eat! The psalmist, repeating the image of the weaned child twice, is helping us note that this is a crucial insight. When we have grown in faith and trust of God, we can be more like the growing child who— still dependent on the mother—can enter into other kinds of relationships: play, tenderness, learning. A more "grown-up" spiritual life doesn't end our need for God, but it allows us to broaden that relationship.

PRAYER

Help me be still and silent,
God who gives me life.
Let me know you more fully
and come to love you more and more.

LIVING THE PRAYER

Today I will act less like a fussy, needy child when I pray.
What words characterize my relationship with God? Does it have different facets? Is it only a reflection of my mood? In what ways can my life in God mature?

THE NEW TESTAMENT SINGS

When I was a child, I spoke like a child, thought like a child, understood like a child; now, a man, I gave up childish ways. (1 Corinthians 13:11)

PSALM 132:8

Arise, O Lord, go up to the place of your rest,
you and the ark of the covenant.

*The whole of this psalm recounts David's promise to God that he
will devote relentless energy to building a temple, a permanent
dwelling-place for God (a project that didn't meet with complete
acceptance in David's time). David was a bit overcome by his
desires for Israel to be like other nations, with palaces and
temples and commerce and armies and geographic stability.
He missed one of the key desires of the God of the covenant: to be
able to dwell wherever the Chosen People were, or wherever they
may have had to go. The resting place that God truly wanted—
Israel's love and fidelity—was intended as a blueprint for their
faith, not their architecture.*

PRAYER

O Lord of hosts,
rest in my heart,
dwell among your people.
Make us your dwelling place on earth.

LIVING THE PRAYER

Today I will work to become a stronger part of God's dwelling.
How am I an "ark" of God's glory? Of God's justice or peace?
Of God's mercy and forgiveness? Do I work with others to be
a "resting place" for God in the world today?

THE NEW TESTAMENT SINGS

And the Word became flesh and made his dwelling among us.
(John 1:14)

PSALM 133:2

Peace is like precious olive oil poured on the head,
    running down on the beard,
running down Aaron's beard,
        down the collar of his robes.

Most of us, if precious olive oil were poured on our heads so that it ran down our faces and onto our clothes, would be reaching for the stain remover. In our religious frame of reference, any sort of anointing rite is done with just a dab. But Israel poured and poured, as a sign of God's lavish love and presence upon those who were anointed for service. Aaron, brother of Moses, is the first to be named "anointed priest" of Israel, another signal in this psalm of what a profound blessing God's peace is: a blessing that completely drenches the first among God's chosen ministers.

PRAYER

Source of all peace,
be with me today;
make me a messenger
of the peace only you can give.

LIVING THE PRAYER

Today I will live as one fully anointed with God's gift of peace.
Do I think that "peace" is a mere absence of conflict? Does God's peace saturate my whole being and every moment of my life?

THE NEW TESTAMENT SINGS

Blessed are the peacemakers, for they will be called children of God.
(Matthew 5:9)

PSALM 134:1

Praise the Lord, servants of the Lord,
who minister through the night
in the Lord's house.

*Unlike modern-day churches that often are locked up after
dark and kept locked through the night, the temple had round-
the-clock ministers at prayer, offering sacrifices and making
sure that the chosen people of the God who neither slumbered
nor slept would neither slumber nor sleep in their own prayer
and worship. This was a pattern that monasteries sometimes
followed, especially during significant times and seasons of the
year (for example, the Christmas watch or Thursday/Friday/
Saturday in Holy Week). We can't individually pray or worship
round the clock, but this can be our model for a daily consecration
of all our time to God.*

PRAYER

God of dawn and daylight
and twilight and nighttime,
keep me faithful to you,
awake or asleep.

LIVING THE PRAYER

*Today I will say several prayers to dedicate myself to God
throughout the day.*
No matter how busy I am, can I take the briefest moments
during my day to reconnect with God? Are there other
ways that I can utilize my time to remind myself that God is
constantly with me?

THE NEW TESTAMENT SINGS

Be alert: you do not know when the master of the house will
come, in the evening, at midnight, when the cock crows, or in the
morning.
(Mark 13:35)

142

PSALM 135:15

The idols of other nations are silver and gold,
made by mortal hands.

*By and large, our society lives in blithe ignorance of its idols.
We may even think it is a good or positive thing to have idols,
or to be idolized; we may even confuse idols and icons. The first
commandment is serious about idolatry—the placing of any
obstacle between us and God. We may not be making golden
calves or statues of Baal or Isis, but it would not be difficult
to name things (possessions, authority) or people (celebrities,
athletes) who receive an unwarranted amount of our time or
devotion, keeping us from tending to our call to do the work of
the gospel.*

PRAYER

One, true, living God,
keep my eyes on you alone,
my heart open to you alone,
every day lived for you alone.

LIVING THE PRAYER

Today I will remove a barrier that stands between God and me.
Can I read scripture instead of a tabloid? Turn off the sports
channel to spend some time in prayer? Do I gossip or conspire
with others, and keep them from living a good disciple's life?
What are the obstacles that I face or create?

THE NEW TESTAMENT SINGS

Therefore, my beloved ones, run away from all idolatry.
(1 Corinthians 10:14)

PSALM 136:26
God's love endures forever.

*The verse citation for this could be any verse of this psalm!
It gets repeated twenty-six times. The prayer form of this psalm
is a litany, in which a response gets repeated over and over.
Sometimes our modern culture doesn't like this inefficiency in
prayer; we've said it, now let's move on to a new thought. But
God's love (or loving-kindness or faithful love or steadfast love,
depending on the translation) of which the psalm sings was the
very heart of Israel's covenant with God. In this psalm it keeps
pulsing and pulsing, just like a heartbeat, keeping Israel's own
love for and faithfulness to God alive.*

PRAYER

Today and every day,
O Lord, may I reflect
your enduring, faithful love for me.

LIVING THE PRAYER

*Today I will stop at least five times to remind myself—or others—
of God's lasting love.*
Is prayer of some sort the true "heartbeat" of my day? Can I
recall a short phrase from a Sunday scripture to consecrate
each day throughout the week?

THE NEW TESTAMENT SINGS

Always keep yourself in the love of God, as you wait for the mercy
of the Lord Jesus Christ to bring you to everlasting life.
(Jude 1:21)

PSALM 137:4
How can we sing the LORD's song
in a foreign land?

The kingdom established by David that continued under Solomon's reign was, in many ways, a high point in ancient Israel's history. They had established a temple for God to dwell in, acquired more land, grown in wealth through commerce, and gained stature in the eyes of neighboring nations. But squabbling and the rise of powerful foes brought all of that to an end, and they found themselves exiled, their temple destroyed, their beloved nation no longer under their feet. No matter where we are, things can feel "foreign" sometimes; we feel disconnected from others, from God, and from our faith.

PRAYER

No matter where I am, O Lord,
you are with me;
I am always a temple
for your Spirit.

LIVING THE PRAYER

Today I will offer God my fullest praise; my whole being is God's dwelling place.
When has daily life felt "foreign" to me? Perhaps others in my family do not practice their faith. Maybe my workplace is hostile to honesty and integrity. Can I remember that God is still with me?

THE NEW TESTAMENT SINGS

Do you not know that you are God's temple and that God's Spirit dwells in you?
(1 Corinthians 3:16)

PSALM 138:1

I give you thanks, O LORD, with all my heart;
I will sing my praises to you
before the other gods.

*The "other gods" make frequent appearances in the psalms.
To those of us who believe in only one God and understand that
Judaism is the origin of this belief, this can get confusing. These
psalms come from a time when Israel didn't deny the existence of
other gods, but denied their worth. Israel sang its praise so fully,
having nothing left to praise other gods, that its fierce dedication
to one God alone made the others vanish. The Spirit still inspires
this lesson for us today: we must devote our eyes, lips, and hearts
exclusively to the praise of the one, true, living God.*

PRAYER

I praise you, my God.
Fill my heart with the joy of your love
so I will desire nothing else.

LIVING THE PRAYER

*Today I will set aside one minute to focus all the energies of my
love on God alone.*
Are the distractions in my life intentional or unintentional?
Are there distractions that take so much of my mind and heart
that they become an obstacle between God and me?

THE NEW TESTAMENT SINGS

Who will not glorify you in awe, O Lord? You alone are holy.
All nations will worship you, for your righteous deeds have been
revealed.
(Revelation 15:4)

PSALM 139:17
How precious to me are your thoughts, O God!
How vast is the sum of them!

In The Lord of the Rings Gollum refers to the Ring as his "precious." Obtaining it becomes the driving force of his existence. We all can name things in our lives that are "precious" to us, if not to this extreme, then to the extent that they are what we give our time, energy, and attention to more than all else. Would "God's thoughts" make that "precious" list? Israel's God was a thinking God. We conceive of God being more than thinking. What do you suppose God thinks about? What is God thinking about right now?

PRAYER
As I think of you today, Lord,
I ask that you conform my thoughts to yours,
so that I may live according to your will.

LIVING THE PRAYER
Today I will make the things of God truly precious in my life. What things do I treasure or cherish most in my life? Are they of God or from God? How do I truly acknowledge this, and live my life to show that it is God who makes these things precious to me?

THE NEW TESTAMENT SINGS
Who has known the mind of the Lord? Who has been made God's counselor?
(Romans 11:34)

PSALM 140:12

I know that the LORD achieves justice for the poor
and upholds the cause of the downtrodden.

There is a certain strength in saying "I know" instead of "I believe." A number of African-American spirituals use this kind of "I know" language, although the slave culture from which most of them emerged presented the singers with an abundance of contradictory evidence. But they had learned the lesson of this psalm verse: No matter what may or may not be happening around us, we must know *how God acts—on behalf of justice for the poor, aiding the cause of the powerless. We must also know that when we act in this way, we are acting as messengers of God.*

PRAYER

I know that you are with me every day,
my loving God.
Let those around me
know your presence by my witness.

LIVING THE PRAYER

Today I will do one thing that will help others know that God is acting in our world.
Can I go beyond just being nice today? Or just doing small courtesies? Is there something I can do for someone—even someone I don't know or don't know well or don't like very much—that will be a God-like action?

THE NEW TESTAMENT SINGS

Jesus said, "When you give a banquet, invite those who are poor, crippled, lame, or blind, and you will be blessed."
(Luke 14:13–14a)

PSALM 141:5

Let the righteous strike me—for that is kindness;
      let the just rebuke me—that is oil on my head.

Most of us are ready to accept a rebuke from God. But are we truly ready to accept—and accept gladly—a rebuke from godly people? Can we think of it as a holy anointing on our heads? When the people we respect or admire correct us, it is a good thing for us to accept it and make some sort of change in our lives. But it is even better to see the voice, or feel the hand, of God at those times and rejoice. The scriptures are always calling us not merely to do what is right, but to become better by doing so.

PRAYER

I am your servant, O Lord.
Grant me grace to allow
those who are righteous
to be your messengers to me.

LIVING THE PRAYER

Today I will search for the hand of God in the deeds of someone trying to help me.
Why do we find a lot of "self-help" in the bookstore, but not so much in the "other-help" section? Do I permit and rely on others to be the presence of God's will in my life?

THE NEW TESTAMENT SINGS

The eyes of the Lord are on the righteous, the ears of the Lord attend to their prayer.
(1 Peter 3:12)

PSALM 142:3

Whenever my spirit grows faint,
you still know my way.
In the paths I walk
they have laid a snare for me.

It's classic movie fare: the lost, lone adventurer walking through the desert sands or the icy tundra who can't go one step further when help arrives or the destination appears in the distance. Or the wanderer in the jungle or forest who is suddenly grabbed by the ankle and snapped skyward to dangle from a tree branch. These scenes appear time again because they are experiences that we, in some way, can identify with—finding ourselves weak and faint, feeling like a trap has been sprung on us. As hard as it may be at those times, the psalmist reminds us, we must not lose confidence in God.

PRAYER

Stay by my side today,
God my hope.
With your guiding touch to lead me,
I will not lose my way.

LIVING THE PRAYER

Today, as I walk or move about, I will spend some time recalling that God always leads me.

We all "lose our way"—literally or figuratively—from time to time. At those times, to whom do I turn? Do I rely on myself, or ask for God's assistance and guidance?

THE NEW TESTAMENT SINGS

Therefore, since you have received Christ Jesus the Lord, walk in his ways.
(Colossians 2:6)

PSALM 143:11

For the sake of your name, LORD, grant me life;
in your justice, rescue me from my distress.

*Through much of their ancient history, Israel lived in a world
where their God was surrounded by other gods. They were surrounded by other nations with many gods, whose presence is
even acknowledged in the first commandment. So from time to
time, Israel would ask God to act in certain ways, "for the sake
of your name," so as not to look bad in front of the gods of the
other nations. For the sake of "the name" was also important
to the first Christians, those named for Christ. They had to act
so others would exclaim, "See how these Christians love each
other!"*

PRAYER

Let me glorify and honor
your name, O Lord,
in the way I treat others
and live my life.

LIVING THE PRAYER

*Today I will do one thing that will make others recall God's
presence when they hear my name.*
"What will people think?" Usually we're told not to be
concerned about this; but for those in a covenant of love with
God, what people think about us matters. Do people think my
life is godly?

THE NEW TESTAMENT SINGS

Peter said, "I have no silver or gold; what I do have I give you:
In the name of Jesus Christ the Nazarene—Arise!"
(Acts 3:6)

151

PSALM 144:2

The LORD is my loving God and my fortress,
my safety and my deliverer,
my shield in whom I take refuge,
who vanquishes my enemies for me.

This psalm is a patchwork quilt prayer: some creation verses, some assurances of bounty, some cries of the warrior. Verse two is a litany (some translations end this verse "who subdues peoples under me"), and it is this way of praying that can serve as a key for all of prayer. This litany serves as a reminder of the many ways God is present in our lives, the many things God does for us, and our complete reliance on God. Like the entire psalm, it calls us to a humble stance before God.

PRAYER

I place myself before you
in humility, Lord God.
Protect me, guide me,
keep me safe now and always.

LIVING THE PRAYER

Today I will name at least ten ways God helps me, blesses me, and continues to grant me life.
As I count my blessings, do I remember the source of all blessing? Do I express my gratitude and acknowledge my complete dependence on God?

THE NEW TESTAMENT SINGS

Jesus answered Pilate, "You would have no authority over me, had it not been given to you from above."
(John 19:11)

PSALM 145:18

The LORD is near to all who call on him,
to all who call on him in truth.

God loves to hear from us. As this psalm illustrates, it is a way for God and us to draw closer to each other. This is the "truth" of calling on the Lord; it must be born of our longing to be nearer to God. Whether we are calling on the Lord for relief from trials, in gratitude for a blessing, or in spontaneous praise, we make it true (or "make it real") if, in calling out to God, we rekindle our desire to be closer to God, until we come to live in the kingdom forever.

PRAYER

Draw close to me, Lord.
You are the God of my life,
who named me for Christ.
Hear me as I call upon your name today.

LIVING THE PRAYER

Today I will truly call on the Lord's name, so we will be closer to one another.
How many calls do I make and receive each day? Are all of them important? What call could be more important than calling on the Lord?

THE NEW TESTAMENT SINGS

Not all who call out to me, "Lord, Lord," will enter the kingdom of heaven. Only those who do the will of my Father in heaven will enter.
(Matthew 7:21)

PSALM 146:2

I will praise the LORD all my days;
I will sing praise to my God as long
as I shall live.

This is the first of five praise psalms (Hallel in Hebrew, source of our "Hallelujah") that conclude the whole psalter. The book of psalms is divided into five parts, in imitation of the five books of the Torah, Israel's law. Praise, then, is their ultimate response to and the crown of God's covenant. Indeed, we will praise God as long as we live, for praising God with the choirs of saints and angels for eternity is what we will do once the praise-filled days of this life are over.

PRAYER

I praise you, O Lord my God.
Let every word and deed,
every joy and sorrow,
my waking and sleeping
be filled with your praise!

LIVING THE PRAYER

Today I will praise God by acting in mercy, charity, or justice. The psalms articulate the love and justice of God, all the things for which God is praised. Do I also give God praise by living in this "image" of God?

THE NEW TESTAMENT SINGS

Why do you judge each other? Or why do you treat each other with contempt? For all of us will stand before the judgment of God. It is written: "The Lord says: 'As I live, every knee will bow to me, and every tongue will render praise to God.' "
(Romans 14:10–11)

154

PSALM 147:4

He determines the number of the stars;
he gives to all of them their names.

*God's numbering and naming of the stars was considered to be
a sign of the splendor of God's power and the depth of God's
love for every created thing. Throughout their scriptures,
the Israelites' names (or name changes) were signals of God's
action; their covenant was continued through the naming ritual
as well. The vastness and naming of the stars was how the
future of the covenant was described to Abraham. So this
passage signals not only God's power as Creator, but God's
faithfulness and love as a keeper of the covenant promise.*

PRAYER

Maker of the heavens and the earth,
in Christ I was named for your glory.
Count me among those you love;
fill me with your light.

LIVING THE PRAYER

Today I will name somebody a "star" in my life.
Have I ever thought about naming a star for someone as a gift?
Might it be better (and cheaper!) for me just to tell others how
they illumine my life with God's light and life?

THE NEW TESTAMENT SINGS

"It is I, Jesus, who have sent my angel to you with testimony for
the churches. I am both root and descendant of David, the bright
morning star."
(Revelation 22:16)

PSALM 148:5

Let them praise the name of the LORD,
for he commanded and they were created.

The creation accounts of Genesis were never far from Israel's
spiritual heart. As a matter of fact, this psalm echoes much of
those accounts in its call to all of creation—on earth and in the
heavens—to praise the Creator. High and low, cold and hot,
dark and light, it impossible to name anything that God did not
create, and so all things are consecrated to God's praise. At the
conclusion of this psalm we are reminded that even the ability to
praise our Creator is itself a creation; God created our ability to
render praise!

PRAYER

Loving Creator of all,
fill me with praise for you. *
Let me listen to all the voices
extolling you in worship,
and let mine join with them!

LIVING THE PRAYER

Today I will praise God by surrendering a luxury or non-essential
thing in my life.
Do I view wise and careful stewardship as a way of giving
praise to God? Is my use of the earth's resources a sign of
my praise joined with the rest of creation, or merely selfish
consumption?

THE NEW TESTAMENT SINGS

Everything created by God is good; we must not reject any of it,
but receive it all thankfully.
(1 Timothy 4:4)

PSALM 149: 6
Let the high praises of God be in their throats
and two-edged swords in their hands.

There's a bit of a mood swing at this point in the psalm, its joyous exultation turned into glowering threats. Ancient Israel was very steeped in the culture of militaristic vengeance and conquest as emblems of God's favor. It isn't all that difficult to find individuals or societies today with that same mindset. But, as we read this psalm to its conclusion, we recall that Christ, though he spoke of bringing "the sword" of divisiveness himself, also showed us how to wield true power: by surrendering himself.

PRAYER
Fill my heart and deeds
with your praise, O God.
Let me remain true to your will,
working eagerly to end all discord.

LIVING THE PRAYER
Today I will speak positively and gently when I would rather cut someone down.
Though I may not wield a real sword, do I still cut others down? Does my self-righteousness masquerade as what God desires?

THE NEW TESTAMENT SINGS
You then, my child, be strong in the grace that is in Christ Jesus; and what you have heard from me through many witnesses entrust to faithful people who will be able to teach others as well. Share in suffering like a good soldier of Christ Jesus.
(2 Timothy 2:1–3)

PSALM 150:6
Let everything that breathes praise the LORD!

When God wanted to give life to a lump of earth, it was with breath. That lump, our human body, can live quite a while without food or even water, but no more than a few minutes without breath. When the Risen Christ wanted to give life to a fearful clump of disciples, it was with his very breath, the Holy Spirit. That Spirit dwells in our re-spir-ation and in-spir-ation to this day. Can we truly live more than a few minutes without the Holy Spirit, heaven's very breath?

PRAYER

Spirit of the living God, my life and breath,
fill me today with your power.
Let me be a good steward of my own breath,
using it to proclaim your word
of justice, mercy, joy, and peace.

LIVING THE PRAYER

Today I will call upon the Holy Spirit, my very breath, and offer my life in service.
We expend a lot of breath each day. Has some of that breath today been in praise of God? In prayer or worship? In a kind word? In speaking out against evil? In being an advocate for the poor or powerless?

THE NEW TESTAMENT SINGS

Jesus said to them again, "Peace be with you. As the Father has sent me, so I send you." When he had said this, he breathed on them and said to them, "Receive the Holy Spirit."
(John 20:21–22)

ALAN J. HOMMERDING

Alan J. Hommerding holds graduate degrees in theology, liturgy, and music from St. Mary's Seminary and University, Baltimore, and the University of Notre Dame, with additional studies in organ, accompanying and vocal/choral pedagogy at Princeton University, Westminster Choir College, and the Peabody Conservatory.

Alan is the editor of *AIM: Liturgy Resources* magazine, a quarterly journal from World Library Publications. His collection of hymn texts, *Song of the Spirit,* and prayers for musicians, *Blessed Are the Music-Makers* (both available from WLP), have received excellent reviews. As a hymn writer, he appears in the most recent edition of *Panorama of Christian Hymnody* and in the *New Cambridge Dictionary of Hymnology.* In WLP's *WorshipWorks* series is his *Words That Work for Worship.* He has been a featured speaker for the prestigious Hovda Liturgy Lecture series for the National Association of Pastoral Musicians, and convenes the music seminar of the North American Academy of Liturgy.

In addition to his editorial work, Alan presents music clinics and reading sessions, hymn festivals, and workshops on liturgy throughout the country. Alan compiled *A Sourcebook about Music* and contributed to *Traditions and Transitions,* both from Liturgy Training Publications. He is a member of the music advisory staff for the Archdiocese of Chicago's Office for Divine Worship, and has served as a faculty member, performing artist, and accompanist for many archdiocesan programs and liturgical celebrations. He has written articles and reviews for *Pastoral Music, Catechumenate, Modern Liturgy, The American Organist, Choral Journal, The Hymn,* and *Christianity and the Arts.*